DEI Conversations Made Easy

Three Easy Steps to Breakthrough Diversity, Equity & Inclusion Conversations with Anybody, Anywhere, Anytime

John E. Mays, "The I Believe I Can Man"

THE I BELIEVE I CAN MAN

Copyright © 2023 by John E. Mays

LEGAL DISCLAIMER

This book, herein referred to as "the Work", is intended to provide general information and guidance on topics relevant to Diversity, Equity, and Inclusion (DEI). The author and publisher make no representations or warranties of any kind with regard to the completeness or accuracy of the contents of the Work and specifically disclaim any implied warranties of merchantability or fitness for a particular purpose.

The advice and strategies contained herein may not be suitable for your situation. You should consult with a professional where appropriate. The author and publisher shall not be liable for any loss of profit or any other commercial damages, including but not limited to special, incidental, consequential, or other damages.

The views and opinions expressed in this Work are those of the author and do not necessarily reflect the official policy or position of any agency of the U.S. government or any other organization.

The material in this Work is subject to change, without notice, due to statutory and regulatory changes, court rulings, changes in accepted professional practice, or other factors.

Neither the author nor the publisher are engaged in rendering legal, accounting, or other professional services. If legal advice or other expert assistance is required, the services of a competent professional person should be sought.

All information in this Work is provided "as is", with no guarantee of completeness, accuracy, timeliness or of the results obtained from the use of this information, and without warranty of any kind, express or implied.

Your use of this Work confirms your understanding of these disclaimers. If you do not agree with these disclaimers, please do not use this Work.

Contents

Book Summary	1
Biography	3
Dedication & Acknowledgements	5
Foreword	6
Introduction	9
Creating Your Personal DEI Perspective	19
Three EASY Steps	37
Step 1 – NO DEFENSE	41
Step 2 – NO OFFENSE	71
Step 3 – NO PENALTIES	113
Appendix	131
AI BONUS SECTION	138

Book Summary

"DEI Conversations Made Easy: Three Easy Steps to Breakthrough Diversity, Equity & Inclusion Conversations with Anybody, Anywhere, Anytime," is an empowering guide that simplifies the complex topics of Diversity, Equity, and Inclusion (DEI). Its aim is to equip readers with the confidence and knowledge to engage in meaningful DEI conversations with anyone, regardless of the setting or time.

This book breaks down the process into three straightforward steps. These steps provide a clear pathway to understanding and discussing the multifaceted subjects of diversity, equity, and inclusion. They include understanding the importance of DEI, learning effective communication techniques tailored to these sensitive topics, and practical ways to apply this knowledge in real-life situations.

Throughout this book, the reader is encouraged to approach DEI discussions with empathy, openness, and respect. This guide emphasizes the need to make DEI conversations easy to understand and execute, making the principles of DEI accessible to all.

By the end of this book, readers will have a solid foundation of DEI principles and will be equipped with the tools to effectively engage in and facilitate these important conversations. Whether you're in a workplace, academic setting, or social situation, "DEI Conversations Made Easy" empowers you to confidently navigate and promote DEI discussions, contributing to a more inclusive and equitable society.

Biography

John "The I Believe I Can Man" Mays is the former Director of Equity and Inclusion for YUM! Brands division KFC U.S. John led the development and implementation of KFC's equity and inclusion vision and influenced the long-term brand strategy for equitable outcomes in franchising, executive leadership, marketing, supplier diversity, and equitable staffing and retention. John led organizational changes that not only raised awareness of equity and diversity issues but developed sustainable policies to address equity from the restaurant level to franchisees and the brand headquarters. John has been a requested speaker, panelist, trainer, and equity consultant for multiple organizations nationally and internationally. John holds a master's degree in business administration from the premier HBCU, Tennessee State University. John is currently a full-time Equitable Business Consultant, Real Estate Investor, and Marriage Coach. John has a passion for making sensitive subjects safe and approachable for everyday people. Mays is heavily involved in the non-profit world, specifically within underrepresented communities, serving as vice president of Master Builders Academy, an organization that helps people build their dreams into businesses, through education in the areas of financial solvency, personal development, and more. John serves as the Board Member of the Kentuckiana Real Estate Investors Association, and a Trustee of Christ Temple Christian Life Center where he is actively walking in ministry and his purpose. John works side by side with his wife Joy helping everyday married couples achieve financial breakthroughs. John and Joy have three wonderful children: John Jr (M), Imani, and Jaywin.

Dedication & Acknowledgements

This book, like everything else I've ever written, is dedicated to my beautiful and incredible wife, Joy Renee Mays. Joy, I am deeply in love with you, and I want to express my heartfelt gratitude for your unwavering support in every endeavor I've pursued. I Believe I Can because you believed in me before I believed in me. You've been there for me every single day, even during those countless hours of Zoom and Teams calls from home when I poured my heart and soul into each person, group, and organization. You've witnessed me at my lowest moments, emotionally drained and collapsed on the ground, and you've lovingly wiped away the tears from my eyes. Whenever I contemplated giving up, you stood firmly by my side, and I'm eternally grateful for that. Your unwavering presence in my life fills me with boundless love and admiration. You are an extraordinary wife, a phenomenal and mighty woman of God, and I adore you beyond words. Thank you for supporting me relentlessly. Without you, none of this would be possible, and I want you to know how much I appreciate and love you. You are God's beautiful gift of inspiration and strength in my life. This book is dedicated to you!

Foreword

Welcome to the DEI Conversation Made Easy community and into a safe place to discover how you can influence the change you want to see in any environment at any time. This journey is designed to simplify and make approachable what has been characterized as challenging, intense, or even divisive. Unity and positive environments are created through individual people who say they are going to lead something greater. You are that leader, and this book is designed to help equip you with the language to help others become conversational in an area that may have been uncomfortable or avoided previously.

DEI conversations have a deeper and more spiritual meaning to some than others, but these are more than just good conversations. When done as recommended by this book, you will find that these conversations can break through walls and barriers that will take you and all around you to the next level in your communication, comradery, connection, and collaboration.

Well, there you have it, my people, I wasn't gonna start off preaching but I'm gonna go ahead and just teach this little piece. Feel free to express it with a little bit more spiritual fire than I normally would in this context. I want you to receive this in your heart in a way that you not only hear and read this book but it also impacts you to go and do.

My friends, we stand at a crossroads, a moment in time where we must open our hearts and our minds to the spirit of Diversity, Equity, and Inclusion, or DEI. These conversations aren't just a luxury; they are a necessity, a divine calling to reach out to one another in understanding and unity.

Now, why, you may ask, is it so essential that we engage in these conversations? Let me put it this way. Just as we are all created in the image of God, each of us is uniquely designed with our own talents, experiences, and perspectives. This is what we call diversity. But if we do not take the time to understand and appreciate these differences, we risk creating a world where only some voices are heard, where only some lives are valued.

Just as the Bible teaches us, "There is neither Jew nor Greek, there is neither bond nor free, there is neither male nor female: for ye are all one in Christ Jesus" (Galatians 3:28). We must extend this principle to all areas of our lives. The heart of God is expressed in our diversity, and we need conversations that allow us to explore and appreciate that diversity.

Equity, my friends, is about justice. It is about ensuring that every child of God has access to the opportunities and resources they need to thrive. It's not about giving everyone the same thing, but rather, about giving each person what they need to reach their full potential. Our world is a beautiful tapestry woven by the hand of God, but for that tapestry to shine in all its glory, every thread, every color, every pattern must be given its rightful place.

Inclusion is about love. It's about making room at the table for everyone, especially those who have been left out or pushed aside. When we invite others into our lives, when we listen to their stories, when we honor their experiences, we are doing the work of God. Our Lord Jesus Christ was an amazing example of inclusion. He ate with tax collectors and sinners, healed the sick and the broken, and loved without condition. By engaging in DEI conversations, we are following in His footsteps, practicing the kind of radical, inclusive love that He taught us.

Remember, when we engage in DEI conversations, we are doing the holy work of building a world where every member of the body is valued, honored, and loved. So let us move forward, not with fear or hesitation, but with courage and faith, knowing that God is with us in every step of this journey.

Introduction

Purpose of the Book – Need for Easy DEI Conversations

One thing that I found from my Fortune 500 experience is that DEI has been presented as so complicated and controversial that good people don't feel like they benefit from getting involved in the conversation. When truthfully, it's when good people stay quiet that bad things happen. Whenever something is complicated and difficult for people, they shy away from it, especially in corporate environments and business environments where it feels like we have so much to lose. I've met so many people with great hearts, great intentions, and beautiful stories who were afraid of sharing who they were or going deeper into learning more about who others were because they were afraid to say the wrong thing or afraid that somebody would say something, and they wouldn't know how to respond.

I found that DEI had been presented in such a way that was so overwhelmingly sensitive that middle managers, directors and even some executives of

Introduction

companies couldn't keep up and never felt like they were doing it right and opt to be quiet supporters vs. embracing their role as transformative leader. Some CEOs and Sr. Leaders as the face of organizations have been professionally prepared to perform in front of large groups and stockholders on how to have impactful DEI conversations, but to the everyday person like you and me, we just haven't received that level of individual executive consulting and guidance. So, we felt called to make this subject accessible so that everyday people can understand these concepts and begin to apply them and impact their realm of influence in a positive way.

So why is DEI so complicated? Because people are complicated. Because fairness is complicated. Because changing culture is complicated. But hey, just because something is complicated doesn't mean we back down, right? In fact, it's often the complicated stuff that's the most worthwhile. So, let's roll up our sleeves, dig into the complexity, and get to work making our businesses, and our world, a place where everyone can thrive.

Through this book, you will learn that I like to keep things straightforward and simple, so let's just dive right into it. You see, DEI is like trying to put together a 1,000-piece puzzle where every piece is unique and holds its own value. We're all individual pieces, with our own experiences, backgrounds, and perspectives. The challenge is figuring out how to fit all these pieces together in a way that creates a beautiful and cohesive picture.

But don't get discouraged! The more you practice these conversations and learn about other people, who they are, and how they like to be treated, the better you'll become at it. And remember, every small step we take towards understanding each other and embracing diversity, equity, and inclusion brings us closer to a world where everyone can thrive. Your corner of the world will never be the same! So, let's take it one conversation at a time, and we can start together with anybody, anywhere, at any time.

It is so important to be mentally prepared. This book is designed to help you prepare ahead of time for the outcomes you want to see. You'll be ready anywhere, anytime to have this DEI Conversation with anybody. Ahead of time, we will take our time to explore your thoughts on who you are and what you want people to see, celebrate, and value about you. Also, we will focus on what you want to learn and know about others so you can positively impact and enrich your whole span of influence.

Introduction

What is DEI?

One of the biggest problems that we have as diversity, equity, and inclusion professionals is the fact that nobody understands what diversity, equity, and inclusion really mean. I gotta be honest there are so many different definitions out there for DEI, DEIB, DEIBJ, EIB, EB, CEI, IE, E, DEI, REDI, IDEA, JEDI, DEIA, READI, EDI… etc. (*appendix). It's easy to get lost and confused in this hot mess. If I hadn't read so many books and been immersed in this topic for so long, I don't know if I would have had the patience to keep up with the wokeness of the acronyms so that I could understand all of them. So, what I've found is that you need to have an easy understanding of what diversity, equity, and inclusion are for conversational purposes. We are Going to use the term DEI because it's easy and most people just call you the diversity guy anyway so why make it more complicated than that? For simplicity's sake, when you have some time, research all those different letters and acronyms and sound like a genius to all your friends. For the purpose of this book and this conversation, we're going to use some very easy language so that we can have real conversations with real people anytime, anywhere with anybody.

Let's start off with a very simple definition of diversity. Diversity means different. Wow, that was super-duper easy let's repeat it diversity means different. The simple concept of diversity is that having different people around is a good thing because when we combine our differences, we produce a better result. Diversity is about how everyone is different and unique. Think of it like a big box of crayons. Each crayon has its own color, and when we use all the colors together, we can create amazing pictures. In the same way, when people with different backgrounds, experiences, and ideas come together, they can make the world a better place. The core concept here is that coming together in all of our differences is a good thing!

Oh, now here comes the most controversial word in all of any DEI professional's life, the word equity. The word equity makes the woke get hyped up, and the agnostics get really tight and sensitive. No matter how we describe this word somebody's going to have a problem with it. So, step one of understanding equity is keeping it simple and easy for you to explain so you can describe it to others without feeling those fear triggers come tingling up your side. Equity simply is about each of us getting what we need to succeed. That may be access to opportunities, networks, resources, and support based on who we are, where we are, and where we want to go. Imagine a race where everyone starts at the same line. But some runners have to run with heavy backpacks or in shoes that don't fit. That's not fair, right? Equity is about giving people what they need

Introduction

to have the same chance at success. For example, some kids might need extra help in school, or some people might need a wheelchair ramp to get into a building.

You would think inclusion would be an easy word because it's based on the word included and I think a lot of times what we've seen is that this is the absolute hardest part about DI. People don't understand inclusion because most of us think we know the word included, so we just stop there and cut off our thinking. For DEI, we will need to go one half-step deeper. We're going to share that inclusion in a DEI context simply means an environment where our differences are seen celebrated and valued. Think about a time when you were left out of a game or a group at school. It probably didn't feel good. Inclusion means inviting everyone to join in, no matter how different they might be.

Together, diversity, equity, and inclusion help us create an environment anywhere, anytime where anybody and everyone is treated fairly, feels welcome, and can be their best selves.

The Importance of Easy

Now, you might ask, "Why is it so crucial to make these conversations so easy?" Well, because the power of these often emotionally deep conversations about DEI lies not only in the words we speak, but in the way we make those words accessible, relatable, and actionable. When we simplify these discussions, we amplify their impact, and we pave the way for a brighter, more inclusive future.

When we start to understand and embrace DEI, it's like we're knocking down walls that have been built over many years. We're challenging old, unfair ideas and beliefs. It's a big job and one that needs kindness, understanding, and clarity.

By making these conversations easy to understand, we make it safe for everyone to join in. We make sure that people of all ages, no matter where they come from or what they already know, can take part. This enables them to bring these discussions into their homes, their workplaces, and their communities. We create a place where everyone is included, where every voice matters, and every point of view is important.

Lack of understanding promotes fear. We lose out on so much value and love from others because of this fear. By making these conversations easy, we release even more power to more people to take positive action and overcome fear with knowledge and understanding. We help them bring these talks into

Introduction

their homes, their schools, and their neighborhoods. We inspire them to become change-makers, spreading the DEI message far and wide. When we make it simple for people to join these chats, we start a spark that can turn into a big fire, lighting the way toward a fairer society.

We can't stress enough why it's paramount to make things easy to understand and execute when spreading a broad message. This concept is at the core of effectively scaling this good work and core to communication itself, and here's why.

Firstly, we are living in an information-saturated world. Everywhere we turn, we're bombarded with messages - on our phones, on billboards, on social media. Our human brains can only process so much information at a time. If your message is complicated or confusing, it's going to be pushed aside in favor of simpler, more easily digestible content. Simplicity cuts through the noise, especially in DEI conversations where there are so many strong emotions at play.

Secondly, when it comes to encouraging action, we want to reduce the barriers to action as much as possible. If your audience has to wade through complex instructions, never-ending acronyms, or convoluted processes (which often include another acronym as a bonus), they're more likely to give up and move on. Making things easy to execute increases the chances that your audience will follow through with the desired action.

Thirdly, simplicity aids in memory retention. We, humans, are wired to remember information that's presented in a clear, concise manner. A complex message with many layers may seem profound, but if your audience can't remember it, it's not going to stick. You want positive DEI conversations and the results from those positive DEI conversations to make a lasting impact. On the other hand, a simple, straightforward message is more likely to be remembered and, crucially, shared with others.

Lastly, simplicity is key to inclusivity. We want our messages to reach and be understood by as wide an audience as possible. By making our messages easy to understand, we ensure they're accessible to people of varying age groups, educational backgrounds, and language proficiencies, and help you have that DEI conversation, anytime, anywhere with anybody.

So, remember, family, we must strive for simplicity and ease in our messaging. In a world of information overload, it's the clear, easy-to-understand, and easy-to-execute messages that rise above the rest and

Introduction

truly engage people to impact everything around us.

As you read through this book, keep it simple. Don't let your passionate desire for change or your fear of being embarrassed get in the way of potentially life-changing conversations. Let us be the ones who rise to the challenge. Let us make these conversations easy to understand and execute. Let us become the architects of a world where diversity is celebrated, equity is championed, and inclusion is the norm. Together, we can change the world, one conversation at a time.

Creating Your Personal DEI Perspective

Inclusion Starts with Me – Am I - Learning to See, Celebrate and Value the Things That Make You Different and Special

This may blow your mind and is counterculture, but before we can be inclusive of someone else true self, we need to take the time to learn how to be inclusive of our true self. All too often, we do this backward, and it leads to a performative version of DEI that's all about managing how others perceive your actions and missing the transformative nature that inclusion is designed to represent. So, you quite simply need to understand how to see, celebrate, and value the things that make you special and different, individually. To really have a great conversation in DEI, you have to lead from a place of truth a place of self-awareness and self-understanding so the best preparation you can do is to truly get to know yourself in a positive light of inclusion. Diversity, equity, and inclusion is an inside-out process, and it truly starts with you. We'll talk in the next section about biases and taking a critical approach to who we are. But for now, we need to dig deeper into what makes us so special. Then, we can take that same curiosity and positive intention that we use to look for what's special and unique in ourselves and apply those techniques to seeing, valuing, and celebrating other people who exhibit different characteristics of diversity than we do.

As we move toward embracing the easy steps to have great DEI conversations, use the following steps to take a better look at who you are and what makes your diverse perspective so special:

1. **Schedule Some Self-Reflection Time and Put It in Your Calendar:** Take time to reflect on your life, background, and experience (the good stuff and the not-so-good stuff). Think about your upbringing, your cultural heritage, your personal values, and your life experiences, and how these things shaped your perspective on what you see in the world around you.

2. **Set Your Mind on the Times You Showed Up as Your Best and Brightest Self:** Those moments when you felt like a superstar where everything you touched just worked out right. Who were you in those moments? Who were you in your superhero moments? Write down a list of the moments in your life where you felt like you were completely at your best. It doesn't have to be a

lot. Come on. Just a few notes to help you frame your thinking around what you think is most important about who you are at your best. Take time to challenge the negative thoughts. When self-doubt or negative thoughts about your diversity arise, challenge them to see the superstar within it.

3. **Write Down Some Elements of Diversity About You That You Believe Are Associated with You at Your Best:** Elements of diversity definitely include race, gender, ethnicity, or age, but it is in no way limited to just those things. Diversity includes such a wide range of differences such as educational background, socioeconomic status, spiritual beliefs, religion, sexual orientation, cultural values, personality type, physical abilities, experiences, even the way you think, and much more. No matter how common or uncommon, it's good to write it down so you have a great base of what elements you represent when you are at your best.

4. **List Your Traits and Experiences:** Write down the qualities and experiences that make you unique. This could include your personality traits, skills, hobbies, languages you speak, places you've lived or visited, your beliefs, and experiences that have shaped who you are.

5. **Identify Your Values:** What principles guide your life? What do you believe in? Your core values are an essential part of your identity and contribute to your diversity.

6. **Reflect on Your Interactions:** Think about how you interact with others and how your perspective might differ from theirs. This can shed light on your unique approach to problem-solving, communication, and collaboration.

7. **Ask for Feedback:** Talk to friends, family, and colleagues. They can provide an outside perspective on your unique traits and experiences. Remember to approach this exercise with an open mind and an open heart.

8. **Take a Few Different Self-Assessment Tests:** There are several online tools and tests available that can help you understand your personality type, strengths, and preferences. Examples include the Myers-Briggs Type Indicator (MBTI), StrengthsFinder, or the DISC assessment. These can provide insights into your individual characteristics that add to your personal diversity.

Remember, everyone exhibits diversity in multiple ways. It is so easy to get into a diverse-off competition in our minds. We begin to feel as though we have to be more different than others to be significant or to stand out in the marketplace. Release the thought that you will be overshadowed by your perceived lack of diversity when compared to others. Comparison and competition kill culture. The goal is not to compare yourself to others, but to appreciate the unique mix of traits and experiences that you bring to the table. Embrace your individuality and remember that your diverse attributes contribute to the richness of the communities and spaces you're a part of.

A JOHN STORY: Ok, now let me take you back, back to a time when I hadn't pieced together my own viewpoint on Diversity, Equity, and Inclusion. What ya'll call DEI, I thought was a joke. I knew I was a Black man. I knew some folks didn't sit right with me: their words, their laughter, their judgment about the people I was raised with, about my roots or culture. And truthfully, that made me feel unheard and defensive and up to offensive. See, people get it messed up. Some think that just because a person exhibits some form of racial or ethnic diversity, that they've got DEI all figured out. But that's far from the truth. Each of us has to take time, look within, and understand our identity and how it links up with the big DEI picture.

But it doesn't stop there. It's not just about who you are, but also about where you want to be, and what you're aiming for. The day I put those two together - my identity and my ambitions - I felt like I'd unlocked a new level. I was empowered, ready to face the world, bold enough to speak my truth, and man, it felt good. From shying away from DEI talk to being out there leading the conversation.

And let me tell you, I've seen the same with so many good people, and now I have had the privilege to guide, counsel, and support them over the years. It's like they were stuck on a repeat until they found their DEI rhythm. So, I'm telling you, don't rush past this step. Don't skip it. Invest some time in yourself, understand your journey, and envision your place in this DEI narrative. It's a journey, but family, trust me, it's one you want to be on.

Recognizing Your Biases

It is so critical that we not only look at all the great things about ourselves and the differences that we exhibit but that we take a critical look at the lenses that shape our perception of the things that are happening around us. We've experienced some good things, we've experienced some hard things, and we associate those good things or hard things with people in groups. Our mind likes to compartmentalize things. Even the easiest conversations about diversity, equity, and inclusion have the power to create positive change. However, if we don't acknowledge our biases, we may unintentionally spread unfairness and unwisely become the thing that we don't want to be. By recognizing our biases, we become better listeners, able to understand and learn from diverse perspectives, making our conversations more effective and meaningful.

We all have a circle of influence, whether it's our family, friends, classmates, or community. By acknowledging our biases, we can foster conversations about diversity, equity, and inclusion within our sphere of influence, inspiring change. Having respectful discussions, sharing our personal growth journeys, and encouraging others to examine their biases can create a ripple effect, making a real difference in our immediate surroundings.

As we seek to spread love in our corner of the world and work towards a fairer and more inclusive society, it is important to recognize and address our biases. These unconscious patterns of thinking can affect how we see the world and communicate with others, sometimes hindering progress toward diversity, equity, and inclusion. By becoming aware of our biases, we open doors to meaningful conversations and become agents of positive change.

Becoming aware of our biases involves looking within ourselves. We need to question our assumptions, challenge our preconceived ideas, and actively seek out different viewpoints. This process helps us uncover hidden biases and address them with humility and openness. I took a test once on recognizing my own biases and was shocked to find what they were. For example, one was being biased toward overweight people and I myself was overweight. I never would have thought that about myself, but once it was brought to my attention, I realized that I was projecting my own insecurities about how I was perceived by others because of my weight onto others. A real awakening!

Recognizing biases is just the first step. To make a difference, we need to take action. Armed with bias awareness, we can challenge unfair practices, support inclusive policies, and contribute to initiatives that promote diversity and equity. By using our influence, we become agents of change, helping to build a more just and equal society.

In our quest for progress and unity, recognizing our biases and engaging in transformative conversations about diversity, equity, and inclusion is vital. By being aware of our biases, we can break down barriers, foster empathy, and actively contribute to making the world a better place. Remember, change starts within our circle of influence, and every conversation has the power to create a lasting impact. Let's embrace the responsibility of confronting our biases, and together, we can move towards a future where diversity, equity, and inclusion thrive. In this world, everyone will feel valued, heard, and empowered.

A JOHN STORY: Ok, my people, listen up. Bias? I didn't even know what that word meant at first. And even after I did, I said to myself, "No, that's not me." I'm telling you; I could pick out everyone else's flaws like it was nothing. But checking myself and taking a hard look in the mirror at myself, now that was a whole different ball game.

Don't get it mixed up though, realizing I got biases doesn't make me a bad person. What it does, though, is make me more conscious and awake. So, now when I'm talking with folks, I'm in control. I see my own biases in action, and I can check myself, even if I feel something crazy about to come out.

And let me tell you, it's made me a better man. People can feel it, when you're genuine, when you're trying to understand rather than just talk at people. And the more I understood about myself, the more folks wanted to be around, listen, and learn. It opened doors to hearing them out, learning about them, about their experiences and perspectives.

Sometimes we mistake people's intent because of our biases. We read their intentions all wrong and end up feeling some type of way about it. But when we take time to check those biases, to think about how they might be affecting our perceptions, it changes the game.

It doesn't have to be formal; it doesn't have to be rigid; it just has to be real, genuine, and authentic to you. Stop being so hung up on perfection and understand that a little self-awareness goes a long way. And when we apply that to our DEI strategy, when we're keeping in mind that it's about no defense, no offense, no penalties, it helps us remember that we're all human. We've all got our struggles. We all got issues, including me and YOU..., so, we have to be less quick to judge the next person and work more on winning together in unity.

I encourage you to invest a few minutes to assess yourself using these free Implicit Association Tests online from Harvard University. Link provided below:

https://implicit.harvard.edu/implicit/takeatest.html

Putting Words to What You Believe – Who Are You (What Framed You and Where Are You Now)

One of the greatest mentors I ever had summed up "How to advance in almost every area of your life" by mastering two questions: who are you? And what do you want?

When we understand these two elements in depth, we gain tremendous power in any conversation any situation anytime anywhere with anybody. Pride and fear start to go out of the window when you have a firm grip on who you are, not just how special you are and all the wonderful things about you, but the things about you that need to improve and the things about you that aren't quite right. There's nothing more empowering than truly understanding what makes you tick, what your triggers are, and what your thoughts on things are. There's nothing more empowering than going into any situation with a feeling of freedom and confidence in the person you are and not being in competition with someone else as we perceive them. The key to this conversation will begin with knowing who you are and putting it into some clear language. Go through the following exercise of self-exploration to be able to put some easy and clear language on who you are, what you stand for what you believe, and in the next section, we're doing deeper into articulating what you want.

Step 1: Reflect on your personal identity.

Reflect on your own identity and write down the characteristics that you believe are foundational to your unique perspective. This includes your race, gender, age, culture, religion, socioeconomic status, sexual orientation, physical abilities, education, experiences, etc... Write down these key aspects of your identity that have shaped your life and worldview.

Step 2: Identify your beliefs and values.

What are your core values? How do they align with the principles of DEI? Write down what you believe about diversity, equity, and inclusion. Here are some prompts to help you:

- What does diversity mean to you?
- Why do you believe equity is important?
- What does a truly inclusive society look like to you?

Step 3: Identify personal experiences related to DEI.

Reflect on your personal experiences related to DEI. This could include times when you've felt included or excluded, witnessed, or experienced discrimination, or learned something new about a culture different from your own. Write these experiences down and reflect on how they've shaped your beliefs and attitudes towards DEI.

Step 4: Envision your non-negotiables in DEI.

This is countercultural but needs to be said. For us to make DEI conversations easy we need to have a real understanding of your truth. What are the things in diversity, equity, and inclusion that you believe are non-negotiable points that you would consider egregious? What's your line, what's the point where you would stand up and fight, what's the point that you think is outside the lines and NOT OK. You have to have a point that you say this is acceptable and this is not acceptable. The line of what you believe down deep and are not willing to move away from is your truth, your non-negotiables.

Step 5: Craft your personal DEI Belief statement.

Based on your reflections, craft a personal statement about your beliefs. This statement is just for you, and you don't have to share it with anyone, but you need it to ground you and help you put language and words to frame your mental picture of your own perspective. The lack of clarity in what we believe leads to confusion, doubt, anxiety, and ultimately avoidance.

Putting our thoughts on paper helps them to become easier to digest and easier to understand, and easier to have amazing DEI conversations, anywhere, anytime, with anybody without fear or self-doubt.

Remember, this exercise is not about getting it "right" but about exploring your own understanding and beliefs. It's okay if your views evolve over time, and they should – that's part of the process.

Very Important Note: Good people, it's time we keep it 100 about something. We got a bad habit of not writing our thoughts down. Our dreams, our goals, our plans, they don't get real until we put 'em on paper. You feel me? You gotta put that pen to work if you're serious about something. Write it down, and stick it up where you can see it daily. Be bold with it.

Too many of us out here acting like having good intentions is enough. Like just thinking good thoughts, keeping them all locked up inside is going to make a difference. Nah, family, that's just not cutting it. If you've got a vision, if you've got a goal, you need to write it down.

Whenever possible, get a pen and a piece of paper, and put it in old-school. If not, type it out, and put it on your phone or computer. Just don't keep it hidden away. Don't shove it off to the side. Words have power and your words deserve better than that. Be brave enough to write it down, make it clear, make it tangible, and make it something you can take action on. That's key if you want to see the person you've described yourself to be truly come to life. Write it down, family. Make it plain, make it real.

Defining Your Personal DEI Vision – (What Do You Want?)

The true secret to unfolding your vision lies not within the narrow confines of self-interest, but in broadening your perspective to embrace a much wider scope of life, extending beyond just you and your kinfolks. Indeed, your well-being and prosperity are of importance, yet fulfilling a profound purpose demands the audacity to build bridges, reaching out to individuals hailing from an array of backgrounds, from all corners and walks of life.

Consider your vision as an invaluable gift, one that resonates with hope, faith, and inspiration. It is meant not just for you, but for all those within your sphere of influence. We do ourselves and those in our sphere of influence a disservice if we have expectations for others with no vision to share. Vision produces hope, hope leads to faith, faith leads to belief and ultimately our beliefs guide our actions.

Defining your personal Diversity, Equity, and Inclusion vision is an empowering step that allows you to actively contribute the changes you want to see in your environment. Here's how you can do it:

Step 1: Identify Your DEI Desires.

What changes do you want to see in terms of diversity, equity, and inclusion in your circle of influence? What does an ideal diverse, equitable and inclusive environment look like to you? Reflect on these questions and jot down your answers.

Step 2: Recognize Your Power.

Understand that you, as an individual, have the power to bring about change. By being aware, taking responsibility, and acting, you can influence attitudes, behaviors, and policies in your sphere of influence. Just by speaking up or refusing to use certain language or participate in discussions will signal to others certain things are not okay and others who might have been afraid to take action now will feel encouraged to do so. As they say, be the change you want to see in the world.

Step 3: Determine Your Role.

What role do you want to play in this change? Are you a facilitator, leading open discussions on DEI issues? Are you an advocate, standing up for the rights of underrepresented individuals? Or are you a mentor, guiding others on their DEI journey? Define your role based on your strengths, experiences, and passion.

Step 4: Formulate Your Vision.

Now that you have a clear understanding of what you want and the role you wish to play, it's time to articulate your vision. Your personal DEI vision should be a concise and powerful statement that captures your desired DEI outcome and your commitment to achieving it.

Example DEI Vision Statement: "I envision a world where every individual is valued for their unique attributes and given equal access to opportunities. As an advocate, I commit to challenging biases, breaking down barriers, and fostering an inclusive and equitable environment in my community."

Step 5: Act on Your Vision.

Once your vision is defined, translate it into actionable steps. This might involve educating yourself and others about DEI, challenging discriminatory behaviors or policies, or creating safe spaces for open dialogue about DEI issues.

Remember, change doesn't happen overnight. It requires consistent effort, patience, and resilience. By investing the time to truly understand your aspirations and desires, you not only establish a stronger bond with your own purpose but also equip yourself with the power to share this vision with others. Standing with conviction in your truth can be a game-changer, transforming the way you navigate through life's myriad landscapes.

The beauty of this journey lies in its transformative potential. As you delve deeper into Diversity, Equity, and Inclusion conversations, you'll discover how they contribute significantly to the maturation of your vision. They enable you to see the world through a kaleidoscope of experiences, enriching your understanding and making your vision more inclusive and impactful. The vision that you cultivate and share, steeped in the values of DEI, becomes a beacon of light, illuminating the path for those around you, and in turn, enhancing the collective journey towards a more equitable and inclusive world.

Three EASY Steps

Three Easy steps to have breakthrough DEI conversations with anybody, anywhere, anytime

Congratulations and Bravo! Give yourself a well-deserved pat on the back! You've successfully journeyed through the essentials, walking through the very foundations of Diversity, Equity, and Inclusion (DEI) conversations. Now, you're prepared to take on the grand challenge of engaging in the three easy steps to DEI conversations anywhere, anytime, with anyone. The stage is set, the audience awaits, and the spotlight is now on you.

1. **NO Defense**
2. **NO Offense**
3. **NO Penalties**

Buckle up and prepare yourself for an exhilarating journey! This is as straightforward as it gets; there are three key steps to mastering the art of DEI conversations: No Defense, No Offense, and No Penalties. Yes, that's all there is to it! But don't underestimate the power of these three fundamental rules. As we continue on this journey, I want you to etch these three steps into your mind, turning them into your guiding principles as we navigate the landscape of DEI dialogues together.

Picture it as the reverse of a sports game. In our DEI discourse, we're playing a different game altogether - one where there is no defense, no offense, and certainly no penalties. There are no teams squaring off, no competition to outdo each other.

Why, you ask? Because the goal here isn't to compete and win, but to collaborate and understand. The victory in a DEI conversation doesn't belong to a single party but is shared when two people can engage with each other openly and honestly. When the playing field is free of combat, free from the fear of ridicule or the dread of being torn down, a psychologically safe space is formed. A space where minds and hearts are actively engaged, working in harmony to create something truly remarkable in the realm of diversity, equity, and inclusion.

In the past, DEI conversations have been mired in trauma, often leading to feelings of insecurity and exclusion. Individuals have been left feeling like they're on the outside looking in, doubting their worthiness to be a part of such significant dialogue. However, today marks the end of that era. As you internalize these three uncomplicated steps – No Defense, No Offense, No Penalties – you are taking a stance for change.

Why these three principles? Because we aren't in a race against each other. This isn't a boxing match. It's not a rumble in the jungle. We're not lining up for the Super Bowl, the World Series, the Tour de France, or the World Cup. What we're preparing for is a meaningful conversation between two people, where the objective is to illuminate each other's perspectives like the dazzling fireworks on the 4th of July (with a nod to Juneteenth), or the joyous celebrations of the New Year or any of your most cherished holidays. We're here to spark a conversation that's as enlightening as it is illuminating, as inspiring as it is insightful. So, let's step into this new phase of our DEI journey with energy, excitement, and a commitment to keep the conversation vibrant, positive, and inclusive!

Three easy steps, No Defense, No Offense, No Penalties. – memorize this!! Remember, keep it simple.

STOP

Before proceeding, make the following commitment to yourself:

I commit to listen without being defensive; speaking without being offensive; and never penalizing the perspective of others!

Step 1 – NO DEFENSE

As we venture further into this exciting realm of conversation, let's introduce the first, yet most critical, of our three steps: No Defense. I can almost hear your thoughts echoing back, "John, what does 'no defense' really mean?" Allow me to clarify. No defense, in its simplest form, means resisting the urge to be defensive.

Why is this so important, you may ask? Defense mechanisms can, and often do, serve as the single greatest hindrance to meaningful, productive dialogue. They are the invisible walls that encase us, limiting our ability to truly connect and empathize with others. Being on the defensive not only stifles conversations but also breathes life into feelings of animosity, anxiety, unease, and fear. It paves the way for avoidance, preoccupation, and, quite frankly, unfruitful conversations that leave both parties feeling unsatisfied and unheard.

Further, defensiveness tends to go hand in hand with self-protection. This is an instinctive response we employ when we perceive a threat or potential harm to our self-concept or ego. But in the context of DEI conversations, it is not our friend. Rather, it

Step 1 – NO DEFENSE

acts as a barrier preventing us from open-mindedly receiving others' perspectives.

One of the biggest moments to focus our attention is not to get offended when someone tells us we are being defensive. If you hear this, take a breath, then choose to believe it. Even if it is just their perception, it is important to listen and evaluate how the things we say are being received. For example: I used to be told in my speaker groups that I was being defensive when getting critiques. I honestly didn't feel that way inside, but something about my body language or my natural inquisitiveness must have been giving that impression, so I had to really work hard on changing that and taking a more thoughtful stance. I found that what I thought was me being inquisitive was really viewed as defensive. For inquisitive people like me, I had to be aware of coming off as aggressively curious and pushing my well-intentioned questions in a way that put others on their heels.

However, there is good news! Over the course of the following section, we're going to delve into a multitude of actionable steps that will guide you to shed these defensive habits. By exploring these strategies, you'll cultivate the ability to engage in open, honest, and impactful DEI conversations. Not only will this serve to improve your own dialogue skills, but it will also enable you to aid others in lowering their defensive barriers, leading to richer and more constructive exchanges.

So, let's embrace this journey of transformative conversations together, armed with patience, understanding, and a willingness to see past our defense mechanisms. Here's to fruitful dialogues and a more inclusive and equitable world, one conversation at a time.

Start Creating a Psychologically Safe Space Wherever You Are (Lead with Your Intention)

Creating a psychologically safe space to have conversations about Diversity, Equity, and Inclusion (DEI) is crucial. This kind of environment encourages open, honest dialogue, fosters mutual respect and understanding, and helps to challenge and dismantle biases and systemic inequalities. Here's how you can do it and why it's so important:

Steps to Create a Psychologically Safe Space:

1. **Establish Ground Rules**: Before starting the conversation, establish a set of rules or guidelines. This may include practicing active listening, respecting differing viewpoints, avoiding blame, and ensuring confidentiality.

2. **Foster Openness and Respect**: Encourage participants to speak openly about their thoughts,

Step 1 – NO DEFENSE

feelings, and experiences, and emphasize the importance of respecting all perspectives.

3. **Actively Moderate**: As the facilitator, it's important to guide the conversation in a respectful and constructive way. This may involve redirecting the conversation when it becomes unproductive, ensuring everyone has a chance to speak, and addressing any inappropriate behavior or comments.

4. **Promote Empathy and Understanding**: Encourage participants to try to understand others' perspectives, even if they don't agree with them. This can help to foster empathy and mutual understanding.

5. **Provide Support**: Be prepared to provide support to participants who may feel uncomfortable or upset during these discussions. This could involve providing resources for further learning or offering to continue the conversation in a more private setting.

Why It's Important:

1. **Promotes Open Dialogue**: Psychological safety allows people to express their thoughts and feelings without fear of judgment or retribution, promoting more open and honest dialogue.

2. **Facilitates Learning and Growth**: In a safe environment, people are more likely to take risks, make mistakes, and learn from them, leading to personal and collective growth.

3. **Strengthens Relationships**: When people feel safe, they're more likely to trust and respect each other, strengthening relationships and fostering a sense of community.

4. **Supports DEI Goals**: By creating a safe space for DEI conversations, you're actively supporting DEI goals. These discussions can help to challenge biases, promote understanding, and drive action toward a more diverse, equitable, and inclusive environment.

Remember, creating a psychologically safe space is a continual process that requires ongoing effort and commitment. However, the resulting open and constructive conversations can have a profound impact on your community or organization's DEI journey.

Important: The moment we forget that individuals are grappling with issues in every facet of their lives - personally, professionally, within their families, and friendships - we lose a part of our empathy. Each one of us carries our unique burdens,

Step 1 – NO DEFENSE

dramas, and challenges that sometimes weigh heavily upon us. I can distinctly recall the time when I was grappling with depression and anxiety; adding another layer of complexity like engaging in a deep DEI conversation was an immense task. As I walked into such conversations, I did so carrying my vulnerabilities, nursing my wounds, and shouldering unspoken realities.

So, it is crucial to foster an environment where individuals, regardless of their personal circumstances, don't feel emotionally attacked or depleted. A space where they can voice their thoughts without replaying the conversation in their minds incessantly, haunted by regret or discomfort. A place where they can interact with you without later lamenting the encounter.

Enhancing psychological safety is a gateway to forging genuine relationships. The more you bolster this sense of safety, the more you open the doors to building authentic connections with individuals. And this, in turn, paves the way for more profound, respectful, and impactful DEI conversations. Because when people feel safe, they can bring their whole selves into these dialogues, enriching the conversation with their lived experiences and perspectives.

Listening Actively and Empathetically

Grandma used to say, "You have two ears and one mouth so we should listen two times more and then, we talk." Still fantastic advice.

If you're anything like me, you might be able to keep your cool for extended periods, standing firm in your convictions. I've found that once I believe I'm right about something, it can be challenging to shift my perspective. My mind tends to latch onto that belief, making it difficult to see beyond it. That's why actively listening - truly hearing with an intention to understand and be influenced - is crucial, especially within the context of DEI conversations.

As a DEI leader, I've stumbled over this in the past. I was entrenched in the belief that everyone else needed to change, without giving much thought to the adjustments I needed to make in myself. Please understand, it's fine to have core principles and strong beliefs, and to articulate them in ways that resonate with people, whether they agree with you or not. But active listening takes things a step deeper.

Engaging in active listening has been transformative for me, granting me a deeper understanding of myself. To actively listen, you need to be open to receiving feedback or perspectives that may not sit

Step 1 – NO DEFENSE

well with you, and sometimes, in ways that may be uncomfortable. These moments of discomfort can stretch your understanding, facilitating change and growth. The real change isn't in our comfort zones; it resides in the spaces that challenge us.

A vital aspect of having fruitful DEI conversations lies in our capacity to listen, to be influenced, and to foster unity and collaboration. This allows us to nurture relationships as we journey together toward a more equitable and inclusive future.

Active and empathetic listening is an essential tool for effective communication, especially when having difficult conversations about topics like Diversity, Equity, and Inclusion. Here's how you can apply it:

1. Pay Full Attention.

Give the speaker your undivided attention. This means not only focusing on what they're saying but also observing their body language and other non-verbal cues. Avoid distractions and make it clear through your body language that you're fully engaged in the conversation.

2. Don't Interrupt.

Allow the speaker to finish their thoughts before responding. Interrupting can make the speaker feel unheard and can disrupt the flow of the conversation.

3. Show Empathy.

Empathy involves understanding and sharing the feelings of others. Try to put yourself in the speaker's shoes and see the situation from their perspective. This can help you better understand their viewpoint, even if you don't necessarily agree with it.

4. Reflect and Clarify.

Reflect back on what you've heard to ensure you've understood correctly. You can do this by paraphrasing or summarizing what the speaker has said. If anything is unclear, ask open-ended questions for clarification.

5. Respond Appropriately.

Once you've fully understood the speaker's point of view, respond in a way that acknowledges their feelings and perspectives. Even if you disagree, it's important to respect their viewpoint and express your own thoughts in a non-confrontational way.

Seek to Understand, Not to Reply:

So many people are just listening for a break in the person's conversation so they can jump in with what they want to say, so they miss the person's true intent. When engaging in hard conversations, it's important to remember that the goal is not to "win" or prove your point but to understand the other person's perspective and find a resolution. This involves:

1. Letting Go of the Need to Be Right

Acknowledge that it's okay to have differing viewpoints and that being "right" is not as important as reaching a mutual understanding.

2. Finding Common Ground

Identify areas where you agree. This can help to foster a sense of unity and cooperation, even when you're discussing difficult topics.

3. Collaborating on a Solution

Work together to find a resolution that respects and incorporates both viewpoints. This collaborative approach can help to strengthen your relationship and promote a more inclusive and equitable environment.

Remember, practicing active and empathetic listening and seeking to understand, not to win, can transform difficult DEI conversations into opportunities for growth, understanding, and positive change.

Asking Open-Ended Questions with a Smile

Have you ever found yourself in a conversation, already determined about where you want it to lead? One surefire way to be defensive in such interactions is to respond with closed-ended questions. This approach hinders the other person's opportunity to genuinely engage or contemplate their responses. Often, they can end up frustrated, feeling unheard, unacknowledged, and unappreciated. This is why it's essential to ask open-ended questions.

And don't just ask these questions - do it with a warm smile, with an inner light, and with genuine joy and thoughtfulness. This requires active listening, but once you've listened, respond by asking a question that probes a bit deeper. Yes, we all have plenty to say, points to make, and visions to share with the world. But in the context of a conversation, the other person is more critical than either you or me.

To facilitate effective DEI conversations, it's crucial to cultivate genuine curiosity about other people's experiences and perspectives. The most potent way to demonstrate this curiosity is by asking open-ended questions. But don't just ask - do so with a genuine smile. For those of us who love to dig deep, our probing questions can sometimes feel like an attack, putting others on their guard. So, always pair your inquiry with warmth in your eyes and a broad, welcoming smile. This approach can shift the direction of your conversations, steering them toward unity.

Asking open-ended questions is a vital tool in promoting productive DEI conversations. These types of questions elicit more than just a 'yes' or 'no' response, encouraging deeper discussion and exploration of thoughts and feelings. Here's how to do it and why it's important:

How to Ask Open-Ended Questions with a Smile:

1. **Be Curious and Genuine**: Approach the conversation with genuine interest and curiosity about the other person's perspectives and experiences.

2. **Frame Open-Ended Questions**: Start your questions with 'how', 'what', 'why', 'where', 'when', or 'who'. For example, "What has been your experience with..." or "How do you feel about..."

3. **Be Positive and Encouraging**: A smile can help create a more positive and comfortable atmosphere, making it easier for others to open up. Keep your body language relaxed and open.

4. **Show Patience**: After asking your question, give the other person time to think and formulate their response. Do not rush them or interrupt.

Why It's Important:

1. **Encourages Deeper Conversations**: Open-ended questions can help uncover deeper insights and emotions, promoting a more meaningful conversation.

2. **Facilitates Understanding**: By asking these questions, you're encouraging the other person to share their thoughts, feelings, and experiences, helping you to better understand their perspective.

3. **Promotes Inclusion**: By showing genuine interest in the other person's experiences and perspectives, you're sending a message that their voice is valued and important.

4. **Builds Trust and Respect**: The act of asking thoughtful questions and listening attentively to the responses can help to build trust and respect. These are key elements in any DEI conversation.

Remember, the goal of asking open-ended questions in DEI conversations is to understand and learn from each other's experiences and perspectives. It's not about challenging or debating, but about fostering empathy, respect, and mutual understanding.

Disarming the Shooter – There Is a Loaded Gun Pointing at You. Don't Give Them Any Bullets - What's A Bullet and What's Not Described?

Imagine this scene - you're in a conversation with someone, and you see their body language shift, their mood change. It's as if they've got a loaded gun aimed right at you, prepared to fire some devastating shots. Sure, our role in these situations is not to arm that person with ammunition. But remember, some people will approach you with the sole intent of picking apart everything you're doing. That's okay! These challenges can't derail the DEI journey just because you're worried about criticism.

The beauty of not being defensive is that you only truly demonstrate this quality when someone's attacking you. The principle of 'no defense' only comes into play when someone else takes the offense. Our character isn't truly tested until we face a challenge. It's easy to remain unruffled when no one's provoking us. Our role, then, is to prepare for potential attacks and arm ourselves not with hostility, but with peace, joy, an engaging platform, an inspiring demeanor, and, most importantly, love.

This 'armed and dangerous' love can help to de-escalate conflicts and remove those metaphorical bullets, fostering peace within the conversation.

Maintaining calm and respect during DEI conversations is crucial. Here are strategies to keep people from escalating during the conversation and how to react if they make a personal attack:

Preventing Escalation:

1. **Establish Ground Rules**: At the beginning of the conversation, establish some ground rules like respecting each other's viewpoints, not interrupting, and maintaining a calm demeanor.

2. **Maintain a Calm Tone:** Your tone of voice can significantly impact the conversation. Keep your voice calm and steady, even when discussing difficult topics.

3. **Practice Active Listening:** Show the speaker that you're listening and understanding their point of view. This can help defuse potential conflicts and show respect for their perspective.

4. **Avoid Trigger Words:** Be mindful of your language and avoid words that might trigger a defensive or hostile reaction.

5. **De-escalate Situations:** If you notice someone starting to escalate, try to de-escalate the situation. This might involve taking a short break, refocusing the conversation, or reminding everyone of the ground rules.

Step 1 – NO DEFENSE

Reacting to Personal Attacks:

1. **Stay Calm:** Don't react defensively. Stay calm, take a few deep breaths, and maintain your composure.

2. **Don't Take It Personally:** Remember that people often lash out due to their own issues or emotions. Try not to take the attack personally.

3. **Clarify and Redirect:** Politely ask the person to clarify their point and redirect the conversation back to the topic. For instance, you might say, "I think we've moved away from the main discussion. Can we refocus on...?"

4. **Set Boundaries:** If the personal attacks continue, calmly but firmly set boundaries. Let the person know that personal attacks are not acceptable and that the conversation needs to remain respectful.

5. **Seek Assistance:** If you're unable to resolve the situation on your own, don't hesitate to seek help from a mediator or a neutral third party.

Remember, DEI conversations can be challenging, but they're also an opportunity for growth and understanding. With patience, respect, and empathy, you can navigate these discussions effectively.

For live demonstrations of these conversations, please visit our website at johnemays.com. Here, you will find practical examples illustrating how these discussions can be conducted in real-life situations.

Stop Running Away. Avoiding Is the Worst Form of Defense

Avoiding conversations about Diversity, Equity, and Inclusion (DEI) doesn't solve the challenges we face. In fact, it often exacerbates them by maintaining the status quo and allowing prejudices or systemic inequities to go unchallenged. Here's why it's important to stop avoiding these conversations and some tips on how to approach them:

The Consequences of Avoidance:

1. **Silent Treatment:** When we don't discuss DEI, we're giving it the silent treatment. This means we're ignoring the experiences and perspectives of people who are affected by these issues, which can foster feelings of exclusion and isolation.

2. **Emotional Manipulation:** Avoidance can also be a form of emotional manipulation, as it often shifts the emotional burden onto those who are most affected by DEI issues. They're left to grapple with these challenges alone, without the support and understanding of their peers.

Step 1 – NO DEFENSE

3. **Perpetuates Inequality:** By avoiding these conversations, we're indirectly contributing to the continuation of systemic inequities. Without open dialogue about these issues, it's difficult to raise awareness, challenge biases, and drive change.

Approaching DEI Conversations:

1. **Acknowledge Discomfort:** It's natural to feel uncomfortable when discussing DEI, especially if you're new to these topics. Acknowledge this discomfort, but don't let it deter you. It's a sign that you're challenging your preconceived notions and growing. This includes not only acknowledging it to yourself but acknowledging it in the person/people you're having the conversation with as well.

2. **Educate Yourself:** Learn about DEI issues by reading books, attending workshops, or listening to podcasts. The more you know, the more confident you'll feel in these conversations.

3. **Practice Active Listening:** When participating in DEI conversations, it's important to listen actively and empathetically. Try to understand others' perspectives, even if they differ from your own.

4. **Seek Guidance:** If you're unsure how to approach these conversations, seek guidance from DEI

experts or mentors. They can provide you with valuable insights and strategies.

5. **Be Patient and Persistent:** Changing attitudes and systems takes time. Be patient with yourself and others, but also be persistent. Keep the conversation going, even when it's tough.

Remember, engaging in DEI conversations is an ongoing journey. It might be challenging, but it's also incredibly rewarding. By embracing these conversations, you're contributing to a more inclusive and equitable world.

A JOHN STORY: Remembering my early days as a DEI leader in a major firm, my mind drifts to certain folks. From time to time, they'd come to me with issues they believed were emergencies. But, I had yet to understand the nuances of these topics and found myself crippled by embarrassment and insecurity. I made the mistake of just acknowledging the person, offering cursory reassurance, but avoiding the real conversation out of fear and insecurity.

One such person, feeling unheard, escalated their issue elsewhere. What was initially a small concern suddenly became a major point of contention within our company. Looking back, I see where I went wrong - I was pleasant, yes. I acknowledged the person and had a surface-level conversation, but I shied away from anything that made me uncomfortable.

Imagine my position. Supposed to be the man with all the answers, the guiding light, but I was lost, not knowing how to navigate the situation. I was wrong, and that's a lesson I carry with me.

Ever since then, I vowed not to retreat from the challenges and the unknowns but rather run toward them. After that point, we saw no escalations. Instead, we experienced a surge in engagement and the perception of DEI throughout our organization rose, as we began addressing each issue in a serious and meaningful way.

The golden rule: if it's important to one person, it needs to be important to you. Many of us have a tendency to shrug something off as unimportant because it might not be an issue for us. We have to remember it's not a complaint, not a whine, not a detriment. It's an opportunity for growth. Quite often, those who make the most noise can turn out to be your staunchest allies and advocates in the mission. So, lean into it, embrace it. Trust me, you'll be glad you did.

What Do I Do When They Know More Than I Do About DEI?

In the ever-evolving and continuously changing world of diversity, equity, and inclusion, it's an absolute certainty that there will always be someone out there who knows more than you do. This is where our role as conversation starters comes into play. We're here to elicit the best of what people know. Then, with grace and agility, we pivot from being the one initiating the conversation to becoming the learner, the one on the receiving end of valuable insights.

Let's face it, folks love to chat, and they love it even more when they get to discuss topics, they're truly passionate about and have a deep understanding of. So, how can we get them to open up about these subjects? The key lies in asking plenty of open-ended questions, not letting defensiveness creep in, and showcasing a curiosity that encourages them to share their knowledge, to help you learn more about the subject at hand.

It's a thrill to learn from those who are deeply passionate. This way, not only do you add their wealth of information to your own knowledge base, but you also forge alliances, alliances that can propel you and your company forward on your DEI journey.

Step 1 – NO DEFENSE

So, it's perfectly okay to not know everything about Diversity, Equity, and Inclusion (DEI). These are complex issues that people spend their entire lives studying and working on. Here's how you can handle such a situation:

1. **Acknowledge What You Don't Know:** It's important to be honest about your knowledge gaps. You might say something like, "I'm not as familiar with that aspect of DEI as I'd like to be. Could you tell me more about it?"

2. **Listen Actively:** Use this opportunity to learn from the other person. Show that you value their knowledge and insights by listening carefully and asking clarifying questions.

3. **Thank Them for Sharing:** Express gratitude for their willingness to share their knowledge. This can help build rapport and show that you're genuinely interested in learning more.

4. **Do Your Own Research:** After the conversation, take the time to learn more about the topics discussed. This could involve reading books, articles, or studies, or listening to podcasts or talks.

5. **Stay Open and Curious:** Approach these conversations with an open mind and a sense of

curiosity. Remember, the goal of DEI conversations is not to "win" or prove you're the most knowledgeable, but to learn from each other and work towards a more inclusive and equitable world.

6. **Adopt a Growth Mindset:** Understand that learning is a process. Having a growth mindset, which is the belief that you can learn and grow with effort and time, will help you remain open and receptive to new information, even when it challenges your existing beliefs.

Remember, everyone starts somewhere, and it's okay to not have all the answers. You can always find the answers, but a little empathy goes a long way. What's important is your willingness to listen, learn, and grow.

Overcoming Pride and Fear

Emotions, particularly, pride and fear, can significantly impact DEI (Diversity, Equity, and Inclusion) conversations. Understanding these emotions and learning how to handle them can lead to more productive discussions.

The Impact of Pride and Fear:

1. **Pride:** Pride can be a barrier to open conversations about DEI. If we're too proud to

acknowledge our biases or to admit that we might be part of the problem, we prevent ourselves from learning and growing. Pride can also make us defensive if our beliefs or actions are challenged.

2. **Fear:** Fear can inhibit these conversations in many ways. We might fear saying the wrong thing, being misunderstood, or revealing our ignorance. There's also the fear of conflict or backlash, or of having to confront uncomfortable truths about ourselves and our society.

3. **Desire for Acceptance:** We all want to be accepted. In DEI conversations, this can make us wary of saying or doing anything that might lead to rejection or condemnation. This can lead to self-censorship, which stifles open dialogue.

Handling Emotional Reactions:

1. **Acknowledge Your Emotions:** The first step to handling emotional reactions is to acknowledge them. Recognize when pride, fear, or the desire for acceptance is influencing your responses, and try to understand why.

2. **Practice Mindfulness:** Mindfulness can help you manage your emotions more effectively. By focusing on the present moment and accepting

your feelings without judgment, you can reduce the intensity of your emotional reactions.

3. **Respond, Don't React:** Try to respond thoughtfully instead of reacting impulsively. Take a moment to think about what you want to say before you say it. This can prevent you from saying something you might regret later.

4. **Seek to Understand:** Approach DEI conversations with the goal of understanding different perspectives, not defending your own. This can help reduce defensiveness and promote open dialogue.

5. **Learn and Grow:** Use these conversations as opportunities to learn and grow. Even if you make mistakes or encounter difficult emotions, these experiences can help you become more understanding and inclusive.

Remember, it's natural to experience strong emotions during DEI conversations. What's important is how you manage these emotions and use them to foster understanding and empathy.

A Great Conversation with A Hostile or Difficult Person

Okay, imagine attempting to talk with someone who just doesn't seem to get it or even acts mean during a DEI conversation. It can be tough, right?

Step 1 – NO DEFENSE

The big thing we have to remember is that what looks crazy to us might make total sense to someone else. Even when they're acting up, we must make sure they feel like we're listening, that we care about what they're saying and that they matter, no matter what.

And here's a tricky bit. As they're talking to us, they might think our ideas are just as nuts as we think theirs are. That's a bit humbling, isn't it? When we put ourselves in their shoes and admit we might be the difficult ones too, something kind of magical happens. We start to see them differently, with more kindness, and that can help them grow and change.

Remember, DEI chats aren't about winning an argument. They're about something way bigger than just you or me. We must always remember that the purpose of these DEI conversations is much larger than us - it is about building a brighter, better, and more unified tomorrow. That takes a lot of humility, but it's totally worth it. So, let's remember to be humble, and let's work together to make a difference.

Encountering resistance during a DEI (Diversity, Equity, and Inclusion) conversation is not uncommon. It can stem from various sources, such as discomfort with the topic, lack of understanding, fear of change, or deeply held biases. Here's how to handle resistance during these conversations:

1. **Stay Calm and Composed:** The key is not to let their hostility affect your emotional state. Maintain a calm and composed demeanor, which can help de-escalate the situation.

2. **Don't Tell Them to Calm Down:** There's nothing more triggering than telling someone who thinks they are explaining something and teaching you something important to "calm down." It can take the other person directly to defense and attack mode and frustrate anything else in the conversation. It is an exercise of love to give people a space to share in a way you may not be comfortable with. Give people space to share their truth and that same grace will lead to someone's breakthrough.

3. **Practice Active Listening:** Show that you're genuinely interested in understanding the other person's perspective. This can help them feel more comfortable and open to the conversation.

4. **Educate Gracefully:** However, be cautious not to come across as patronizing or condescending. Share information in a way that invites discussion rather than dictating beliefs.

Step 1 – NO DEFENSE

5. **Ask Open-Ended Questions:** Encourage the person to elaborate on their thoughts and feelings. This can lead to deeper understanding and may help to uncover the root of their resistance.

6. **Assume Positive Intent in Misunderstandings:** Use simple, relatable examples to illustrate your points.

7. **Acknowledge Their Feelings**: Recognize and validate the emotions behind the resistance. Saying something like, "I understand that this might feel uncomfortable for you," can make the person feel heard and more open to dialogue.

8. **Provide Information and Resources**: Sharing articles, books, or videos on DEI can help broaden the person's understanding and potentially reduce their resistance over time.

9. **Know When to Take a Break**: If the conversation becomes too heated or unproductive, it's okay to take a break and revisit the topic later. Sometimes, people need time to process the information and their emotions.

10. **Seek Help If Needed**: If the resistance is significant, you might consider involving a third

party such as a mediator or a DEI expert to facilitate the conversation.

11. **Speak with Empathy:** Always express empathy and understanding in your responses. Recognize that their views might come from a place of misinformation or lack of exposure to diversity.

12. **Use 'I' Statements:** Communicate your perspective without blaming or attacking them. For instance, say, "I feel that..." or "In my experience..." instead of "You're wrong about...".

13. **Encourage Questions:** Inviting them to ask questions can show that you're open to discussion and interested in their understanding. This can also make it easier to explain your viewpoint.

14. **Find Common Ground:** Look for areas where you both agree. This can make the conversation less confrontational and more collaborative.

15. **Set Boundaries:** If the conversation becomes too heated or disrespectful, it's important to set boundaries. You can say something like, "I value this discussion, but I think it's important we treat each other with respect."

Remember, change often comes with resistance, and it's part of the process toward understanding

Step 1 – NO DEFENSE

and embracing DEI. Staying patient, understanding, and consistent can help overcome this resistance over time.

Remember once again, not every conversation will lead to an immediate change in a person's mindset or behavior. But by showing patience and understanding, you're increasing the chances of creating a positive impact.

Step 2 – NO OFFENSE

Alright, let's dive into the second critical component of our DEI conversational blueprint: No Offense. Having grasped the concept of 'No Defense', we're ready to explore how not to be offensive or on the attack during DEI conversations. Let's acknowledge that a significant hurdle exists when we aim to communicate information that the recipient might struggle to accept. So, 'No Offense' isn't just about avoiding inflammatory language, not resorting to foul words, or shouting angrily at someone - it's a deeper concept. It's about learning to de-escalate situations, disarming potential conflict, and guiding the other person to receive ideas without going on the defense. That's where the beauty lies. It takes a awareness to show grace; people have such ingrained beliefs that they don't even realize how insensitive they are, especially if most people in their circle also hold similar beliefs.

Imagine a world where offensive behavior doesn't trigger defensive reactions - that's our goal here. So, we need to assess whether our behavior is leading the other party to adopt a defensive stance. If that's the case, it indicates we've taken an offensive

Step 2 – NO OFFENSE

approach, which we're striving to eliminate. 'No Offense' entails managing our emotions skillfully, and maintaining control even when we feel provoked.

'No Offense' requires us to cultivate a certain level of emotional intelligence and resilience. It means trusting and believing in the positive intentions of others, even when their words or actions may seem to suggest otherwise. It means stepping up, taking the high road, and demonstrating a level of maturity that fosters constructive dialogue.

'No Offense' embodies the idea that no matter where we are, no matter who we're engaging with, we strive to be the bigger person in the conversation. It urges us not to set unrealistic expectations of others based on their positions or the institutions they represent. After all, we're all humans with our unique sets of emotions, thoughts, and feelings.

Our primary objective in adhering to the 'No Offense' rule is to ensure that the other person feels comfortable, is disarmed, and doesn't feel the need to be on the defense. Because offense and defense breed division and our mission is to prevent sides from forming. We aim to facilitate a conversation devoid of competition, a conversation that doesn't favor any side but fosters an open, engaging exchange where you set the tone and steer the energy.

So, even if you feel a tad frustrated, remember your commitment to this approach. You have the tools and the understanding to control your reactions and keep any offensive behavior at bay. So, gear up, embrace the 'No Offense' mentality, and prepare to lead inspiring, transformative DEI conversations!

No Assumptions (Offense)

You might wonder why, in this realm of avoiding offense and being unoffensive, we start by making no assumptions. The reason is simple: assumptions lie at the heart of many misunderstandings, arguments, conflicts, and disagreements.

When we make assumptions about the intent or meaning behind someone's words, it immediately triggers a response. This could manifest in our facial expressions, our body language, or our words, and it's based on what we've assumed or understood from the other person's statement.

To effectively engage in DEI conversations, we must challenge our assumptions. If I presume that your race, gender, or lifestyle preference determines your beliefs, then my assumption about your mindset is making me the very person I'm striving not to be.

Assumptions about individuals and groups form the foundation of every imaginable "ism" (racism, sexism, ageism, ableism. Thus, we must challenge our assumptions and, in a gentle and graceful manner, seek to understand those of others.

Making assumptions in a DEI (Diversity, Equity, and Inclusion) conversation can indeed be detrimental. Here's why it's essential to avoid assumptions:

1. **Assumptions Trigger Biases:** Assumptions are often rooted in our biases. They can shape our perception of others and lead us to make unfair or inaccurate judgments. For example, assuming that someone doesn't understand DEI because they come from a certain background can limit their contribution and create an unnecessary divide.

2. **Self-Protective Behaviors:** Assumptions can trigger self-protective behaviors, which can be aggressive or offensive. If we assume that someone is going to criticize or attack us, we may adopt a defensive stance, which can escalate tensions and hinder open dialogue.

3. **Limits Understanding:** By making assumptions, we limit our ability to truly understand the other

person's perspective. It prevents us from asking questions and gaining insights into their experiences and viewpoints.

4. **Hinders Inclusion:** Assumptions can lead to stereotyping, which hinders inclusion. It's essential to treat each person as an individual with unique experiences, perspectives, and contributions.

To avoid making assumptions:

1. **Approach with an Open Mind:** Start each DEI conversation with the mindset that you have something to learn from the other person. This can help to counteract any preconceived notions or biases.

2. **Ask Questions:** If you're unsure about something, ask. Questions show that you're interested in understanding the other person's perspective and are open to learning. If you demonstrate that you genuinely care, if you do accidentally make an offensive statement; people are more likely to gently correct you and continue the conversation.

3. **Practice Active Listening:** Focus on what the person is saying instead of formulating your response or making judgments. This can help

you to better understand their viewpoint and reduce the likelihood of making assumptions.

4. **Check Your Assumptions:** If you find yourself making an assumption, pause and ask yourself why. Reflecting on the source of your assumptions can help you to challenge and overcome them.

Remember, DEI conversations are about understanding and celebrating our differences, and this requires openness, curiosity, and a willingness to challenge our assumptions.

No Generalizations (Offense)

There exists a strong tendency to overemphasize and generalize behaviors that confirm stereotypes, particularly negative ones, about individuals who belong to an outgroup - a social group to which we ourselves do not belong. We must scrutinize how and when we use these generalizations because they can swiftly become offensive and aggressive to others. It's all too easy to assign negative traits to an entire group based on one or two instances.

Consider this: You have one friend who embodies a certain aspect of diversity. You then generalize that all people who share that diversity trait behave in the same way as your one friend. This approach is flawed. It's an offensive assumption to believe that we understand everything about a whole group of people based on a few isolated examples.

Furthermore, these generalizations often give rise to assumptions. Regardless of whether these assumptions are positive or negative in our minds, they can easily offend others. So, be cautious about how you generalize and shift your thinking from individuals to entire populations, as this can be counterproductive in a DEI conversation.

Using generalizations in a DEI (Diversity, Equity, and Inclusion) conversation can be very counterproductive. Here's why it's crucial to avoid generalizations:

1. **Generalizations Oversimplify:** By nature, generalizations oversimplify complex issues. They reduce individuals to broad categories, ignoring the diversity of experiences and perspectives within those categories.

2. **Promote Stereotypes:** Generalizations often reinforce stereotypes, which can perpetuate bias and misunderstanding. For instance, saying "All people from X group behave this way" is not only factually incorrect, but it also reinforces harmful stereotypes.

3. **Trigger Defensive Responses:** When people feel they're being unfairly lumped into a group, they're likely to become defensive. This can lead to negative emotional responses, aggression, and a breakdown in communication.

4. **Hinder Authentic Understanding:** Generalizations can prevent us from understanding the unique experiences and perspectives of individuals. In DEI conversations, it's essential to appreciate people as individuals, not as members of a monolithic group.

To avoid generalizations:

1. **Speak from Personal Experience:** Instead of making broad statements, speak from your own experiences and perceptions. Use "I" statements, such as "In my experience..." or "I have noticed...".

2. **Ask Open-Ended Questions:** Asking open-ended questions encourages others to share their unique perspectives and experiences, promoting understanding and reducing the need for generalizations.

3. **Acknowledge Diversity Within Groups:** Recognize that every group is diverse and people within it can have vastly different experiences and perspectives.

4. **Be Mindful of Language:** Be aware of the language you use and avoid phrases that group people together in a broad or stereotypical way.

Remember, the goal of DEI conversations is to foster understanding and inclusion, which requires recognizing and respecting individual experiences and perspectives. Avoiding generalizations is an essential part of this process.

Be Overtly Nice and Respectful

Many of us are nice people and think of ourselves as being known as a nice and respectful person. We are all pretty nice when it's convenient with the goal is to be nice when it's inconvenient, when it's challenging, when people aren't very nice to us, or we feel offended in some way. Being nice and overtly respectful is fundamental to any conversation, but it holds special importance in DEI (Diversity, Equity, and Inclusion) conversations given their sensitive and personal nature. Here are some steps to ensure you maintain respect and kindness during these discussions:

1. **Use Polite Language:** Always address the other person in a respectful manner. Avoid using language that could be seen as disrespectful or offensive.

Step 2 – NO OFFENSE

2. **Listen Actively:** Show genuine interest in what the other person is saying. Avoid interrupting or dismissing their points. Active listening indicates that you value their opinion and are open to learning from them.

3. **Be Mindful of Tone:** How you say something is just as important as what you say. Maintain a calm, friendly tone of voice, even when discussing difficult topics.

4. **Respect Different Perspectives:** Remember that people have different experiences and viewpoints. Be open to these differences, and do not dismiss or belittle them.

5. **Avoid Assumptions and Stereotypes:** Treat each person as an individual. Don't make assumptions about their experiences or viewpoints based on their identity.

6. **Be Sensitive to Cultural Differences:** Be aware that cultural norms and communication styles can differ greatly. What's considered polite in one culture may not be in another.

7. **Apologize If Necessary:** If you accidentally say something offensive or hurtful, apologize promptly and sincerely. This shows your respect for the person and your commitment to improving.

8. **Lead with Empathy:** Try to understand the other person's feelings and experiences. This can help you respond in a thoughtful and considerate way.

Remember, DEI conversations can be emotionally charged and complex. By treating everyone with kindness and respect, you can help to foster a more open and constructive dialogue.

A JOHN STORY:

As a seasoned DEI professional, my role often required me to navigate through complex situations and conflicts that were not directly correlated to the space of DEI, but needed the same skillset of connection, equity building and creating unity. One incident stands out in my memory, highlighting the transformative power of simple kindness, respect and being nice.

There were two teams within our company that had been at odds for months. The issue at hand was a significant project; both teams had different visions, and the tension had escalated to a level where it was starting to affect their productivity. They were locked in a power struggle, each feeling unheard and unappreciated by the other.

I felt a responsibility to mediate and find common ground. I decided to approach the situation with a deliberate focus on being overtly nice and respectful. It wasn't about favoring one side over the other, but about fostering a space where everyone felt valued and heard.

I called for a joint meeting between the leaders of the two teams. As we all gathered, I could feel the tension in the room. I began by acknowledging the elephant in the room, expressing my understanding of their frustrations, and the importance of their work to our company.

Then, with a smile, I requested each person to share something positive they had observed in a member of the other team. There were surprised looks and hesitant starts, but gradually, people began to break the ice. It was a small step, but it helped to diffuse the hostility, at least for the moment.

Over the next few weeks, I made it a point to maintain this atmosphere of overt kindness and respect. I set up more collaborative spaces and activities that encouraged interaction between the two teams. I made sure to model the behavior I wanted to see, consistently using respectful language, and taking time to listen carefully to all viewpoints.

Slowly but surely, things started to change. Conversations became less heated, and individuals began to see beyond their differences. They started appreciating each other's strengths and even started brainstorming collectively to find a mutually beneficial solution for the project.

In the end, not only was the project a success, but the relationships between the two teams improved significantly. They now understood the value of diverse perspectives and the importance of maintaining respect, even in the face of disagreements.

My overt niceness and respectfulness helped to create a platform where hostility could be replaced with understanding. This experience reemphasized to me that as a DEI leader, sometimes it's the simple acts of kindness and respect that can make the biggest difference in fostering a healthy, inclusive environment.

Be Vulnerable

Oh, how noble it is to be so confident and so transparent and demonstrate so much openness that you can go into any room anytime anywhere with anybody and be able to give freely from the depths of your soul and to be able to receive the same way. The amount of mental fortitude that it takes to be open to influence is the same courage that it takes to end wars in men's relationships and unite in equity and inclusion conversations.

Brené Brown, a renowned research professor and bestselling author, has emphasized the power of vulnerability in all aspects of life, including DEI (Diversity, Equity, and Inclusion) conversations. She's constantly reminded us about the fact that vulnerability is courage, and it is bravery at its core. Demonstrating a willingness to be vulnerable disarms other people and arms you with love humility and a transformational mindset that is sure to make your DE conversations go to a deeper and more fulfilling level.

Here's why vulnerability is so crucial:

1. **Fosters Authenticity:** By being vulnerable, we show up as our true selves. It means we are willing to discuss our experiences, thoughts, and feelings, even when they are uncomfortable or imperfect. This authenticity fosters trust and connection.

2. **Encourages Empathy:** When we are vulnerable, we create a space for empathy. It allows others to see their own experiences and feelings reflected in us, promoting understanding and compassion.

This is particularly important in DEI conversations, where understanding diverse perspectives is vital.

3. **Invites Others to be Vulnerable:** When we model vulnerability, we signal to others that it's safe for them to do the same. This can lead to deeper, more meaningful conversations.

4. **Promotes Learning and Growth:** Vulnerability involves admitting that we don't know everything and that we make mistakes. This openness can foster learning and growth, both crucial to understanding and promoting DEI.

5. **Challenges Stereotypes and Biases:** Being vulnerable often means sharing personal stories and experiences that challenge stereotypes and biases. This can be a powerful tool for promoting DEI.

In the words of Brené Brown, "Vulnerability is not winning or losing; it's having the courage to show up and be seen when we have no control over the outcome." This concept is particularly relevant in DEI conversations, where vulnerability can lead to greater understanding, connection, and inclusivity.

When a person is not demonstrating vulnerability during a DEI (Diversity, Equity, and Inclusion) conversation, it can manifest in several ways:

Step 2 – NO OFFENSE

1. **Being Defensive:** Instead of being open to new ideas or perspectives, they may become defensive when their views are challenged. They might argue or dismiss others' experiences or insights, rather than seeking to understand them.

2. **Avoiding Difficult Topics:** If they are unwilling to be vulnerable, they might avoid topics that are uncomfortable or difficult to discuss. They may steer the conversation towards safer topics, thereby missing an opportunity for deeper understanding and growth.

3. **Withholding Personal Experiences:** Vulnerability often involves sharing personal experiences, feelings, and thoughts. If they're not being vulnerable, they might stick to discussing abstract ideas or other people's experiences, rather than their own.

4. **Not Acknowledging Mistakes or Misunderstandings:** A crucial part of vulnerability is being able to admit when you're wrong or when you don't understand something. If they're not demonstrating vulnerability, they may insist they're right or pretend to understand something they don't.

5. **Showing No Emotional Engagement:** DEI conversations can be emotionally charged. If they

are not being vulnerable, they might appear detached or unemotional, which can create a barrier to genuine connection and understanding.

6. **Remaining Silent:** Sometimes, not being vulnerable can look like silence. They might choose not to participate in the conversation at all, thereby avoiding the potential discomfort of vulnerability.

Remember, vulnerability is a strength, not a weakness. It's a key component of meaningful DEI conversations, fostering empathy, connection, and understanding.

Peace In Two Words "I'm Sorry"

In any conversation, especially within the scope of Diversity, Equity, and Inclusion (DEI) discussions, the phrase "I'm sorry" holds an incredible power. These simple, yet profound words serve as a bridge, seamlessly connecting disparate perspectives, cultures, experiences, and beliefs. They offer an explicit demonstration of understanding, empathy, and respect, which are absolutely essential to the fabric of any DEI conversation.

In the grand scope of human interaction, there are few things more beautiful, more touching, than a genuine, heartfelt apology expressed in the moment. The act of saying "I'm sorry" has an almost magical capacity to kindle warmth within us, to make us feel cherished, loved, and embraced. An apology, when offered sincerely, can effectively dismantle walls of misunderstanding and resentment that may have been built over time.

However, it's equally important to note that the absence of an apology can result in an impenetrable guard, a fortress of resistance that might be difficult to tear down. That's why apologies hold such transformative power, becoming a catalyst for meaningful change and a beacon of hope for a more understanding future. It's in these instances that sincere, heartfelt apologies can penetrate areas that even actions may fail to reach.

In combining these two aspects, it becomes apparent how essential it is to master the art of the sincere apology in DEI discussions. Through this simple, yet powerful gesture, we can begin to build bridges of understanding and empathy, forging a path toward a more inclusive, equitable world.

Let's delve deeper into why "I'm sorry" is so critical:

1. **Demonstration of Empathy:** Apologizing signifies that you acknowledge the other person's feelings and experiences. It shows that you are empathetic and that you understand they may have been hurt or offended, even if you may not fully comprehend why.

2. **Acknowledgement of Mistakes:** Saying "I'm sorry" is a recognition that we are all human, and we all make mistakes. In the DEI context, this could mean unintentional microaggressions, bias, or misunderstandings. Apologizing shows that you are aware that you may have erred and are ready to correct and learn from your actions.

3. **Creates Psychological Safety:** An apology can defuse tension and prevent escalation. It fosters a sense of psychological safety, which is essential in any DEI conversation. When people feel safe, they are more likely to engage in the dialogue, share their experiences, and be open to understanding others' perspectives.

4. **Encourages Open Dialogue:** By apologizing, you demonstrate your willingness to listen

and understand, promoting open and honest discussion. This attitude is crucial in DEI conversations, as it encourages people to express their thoughts and feelings without fear of criticism or dismissal.

5. **Fosters Trust:** Apologies build trust. When you apologize, you show accountability for your actions, which can strengthen relationships and enhance mutual respect.

So, even if you don't fully understand why the other person is offended, an apology can be a potent tool. It shows your commitment to the DEI conversation, commitment to understanding and learning, and to creating an environment of respect and inclusion. Ultimately, it's not about always being right. It's about being open, respectful, and understanding. That's where the magic of DEI truly happens.

A JOHN STORY:

As a DEI leader I've always strived to foster an environment of respect and equality. Yet, there was a moment when even I, despite my best intentions, fell short.

I was in a meeting when it happened. A fellow leader casually referred to Shameka, a prominent Black woman leader, as "sweetheart." At the moment, it slipped past me, drowned in the midst of our intense discussions.

After the meeting, as I mulled over the day, it hit me. Those words and the casual dismissal of her professional status was inappropriate. I realized I had witnessed a microaggression, a subtle act of disrespect. Worse, I had not said anything, missing an opportunity to support Shameka and set an example of the values we hold dear in our company.

Resolving to rectify my lapse, I first sought out Shameka. I found her in her office, engrossed in her work. I apologized for not addressing the issue immediately and assured her that her experiences and feelings were valid, that such behavior was not in line with our company's culture of respect and professionalism.

Shameka appreciated the acknowledgement and voiced her own discomfort about the incident. Together, we decided on a course of action. I would call another meeting, creating space for Shameka to express her feelings and thoughts to the group.

Gathering the team once again, I started the conversation. I addressed the previous incident without placing blame, highlighting it as a learning opportunity for everyone. Shameka, with the floor open to her, spoke with a grace and power that left a lasting impression on all of us. She calmly explained how such seemingly minor offenses could undermine a person's professional credibility and contribute to an uncomfortable work environment.

Her words sparked a broader discussion about respect and gender equality in the workplace. We all left the meeting with a renewed understanding of the importance of our words and the impact they have on others.

Inspired by the way Shameka handled the situation, several other women in the company approached her, eager to learn from her experience and leadership. Recognizing this potential, we formed a Women's Employee Resource Group, with Shameka as the lead.

In her new role, Shameka leveraged her influence to foster a community that educated, supported, and empowered the women in our company. Today, she continues to be a beacon of leadership, inspiring us all with her strength and wisdom. This experience served as a reminder for me that the work of DEI is an ongoing process, filled with learning and growth for everyone involved.

Verbalize Compliments on Things That Deserve Compliments

Verbalizing compliments and positive affirmations play a crucial role in fostering productive DEI (Diversity, Equity, and Inclusion) conversations. Here's why:

1. **Builds Trust and Rapport:** Compliments can help establish a positive and respectful environment, essential for sensitive DEI discussions. When people feel appreciated and valued, they are more likely to open up and engage in meaningful dialogue.

2. **Affirms and Validates Experiences:** When you compliment someone on their insights, experiences, or the way they've handled a difficult situation, it validates their experiences. This can make them feel heard and understood, which is crucial in DEI conversations.

3. **Encourages Participation:** Compliments can serve as positive reinforcement, encouraging further participation. This is particularly important in DEI

conversations, where diverse perspectives and experiences are crucial.

4. **Promotes Positivity:** DEI conversations can often involve discussing difficult, sensitive, or uncomfortable topics. Compliments can help maintain a positive tone, making these discussions more manageable and less confrontational.

5. **Boosts Confidence:** Compliments can boost the recipient's confidence, making them more comfortable sharing their thoughts, experiences, and feelings.

However, it's important to note that compliments should be genuine and relevant. Hollow or off-topic compliments can come across as insincere and may have the opposite effect. Always strive to be authentic and considerate in your compliments.

A JOHN STORY: In the middle of building out some new DEI initiatives for our company, we began with a huge listening tour, after hearing that we needed more understanding of DEI at all levels, among many other initiatives we began doing some workshops as requested by our community. A seasoned software developer named Greg was known for resisting DEI (Diversity, Equity, and

Inclusion) initiatives within his company, believing solely in the merit of his own skills and everyone else should just focus on work and performance vs. who or what you think in your personal life. Then, during a company workshop, I highlighted Greg and acknowledged Greg's problem-solving expertise in front of the group, and then proceeded to invite him to amplify his ideas and use his talents to help shape the analysis of how we reconcile DEI data and help bring out the unique skills and perspectives of others on our team and in our company. This simple, respectful compliment became a turning point for Greg. Greg wasn't expecting to be complimented and acknowledged; that gentle and tactful approach in a DEI conversation shifted his perspective, transforming him from a skeptic into an active participant in the company's DEI efforts, proving how powerful mindful, inclusive communication can be. He became one of the biggest allies, all based on a compliment and showing some love.

Pre-Frame Your Perspective- Using Emotionally Thoughtful, Direct, and Authentic Language at The Moment.

One of the key aspects of successful communication, especially in a learning or teaching environment, is

Step 2 – NO OFFENSE

the concept of 'pre-framing'. Understand this - no one, absolutely no one, appreciates being caught off guard. People generally don't respond well to being suddenly confronted with information, leaving them feeling unprepared, embarrassed, and as though their interests and needs were ignored. This experience can be particularly jarring for those who are meticulous, detail-oriented, or analytical.

Pre-framing serves as a thoughtful, considerate act that sets the stage for upcoming discussions or information. It equips individuals with a mental preview, allowing them to prepare their responses and engage more effectively. If we neglect this crucial step, if we fail to provide adequate context to our discourse, it may come across as offensive or insensitive. This is particularly true in complex areas like Diversity, Equity, and Inclusion (DEI). By utilizing pre-framing, we can ensure a more open, respectful, and effective communication environment.

Pre-framing is a communication technique where you set the stage or context before starting a discussion. It involves expressing your intentions, feelings, or perspectives upfront to guide the understanding and expectations of the listener. In the context of DEI (Diversity, Equity, and Inclusion) conversations, pre-framing can be particularly important for several reasons:

1. **Sets Expectations:** Pre-framing helps set the tone and expectations for the conversation. By sharing your perspective upfront, you provide a context that can guide the conversation in a productive direction.

2. **Promotes Understanding:** By pre-framing your perspective, you give others a better understanding of where you're coming from. This can help prevent misunderstandings or misinterpretations.

3. **Encourages Openness:** When you openly share your perspective at the beginning of a conversation, it can encourage others to do the same. This openness can lead to more authentic and meaningful dialogue.

4. **Prevents Defensiveness:** If you express your intentions or feelings upfront, it can help prevent others from becoming defensive. By stating that your goal is understanding and not confrontation, you can create a more comfortable and constructive conversation environment.

5. **Fosters Empathy**: By sharing your feelings or experiences at the start of the conversation, you give others an opportunity to empathize with your perspective. This empathy can help build a stronger connection and mutual understanding.

Step 2 – NO OFFENSE

So, for instance, a pre-frame in a DEI conversation might look like this: "Before we start, I want to say that I'm here to learn and understand, not to argue or prove a point. My experience with these topics might be different from yours, and that's okay. I believe that by sharing our unique perspectives, we can learn from each other and grow together."

The Power of "I"

The practice of employing 'I' statements rather than 'You' statements form a significant cornerstone in promoting Diversity, Equity, and Inclusion (DEI) conversations. By beginning your sentences with "I", you inherently avoid placing blame or casting accusations onto the other person. Instead, you focus on expressing your own thoughts and feelings. For instance, saying "I feel upset when..." is a much more effective approach to communication than accusingly stating "You always...". This subtle shift in language usage is vital in creating a respectful and open environment that facilitates constructive conversation.

In the realm of DEI discussions, where the topics at hand are often sensitive and highly personal, avoiding an attack-oriented dialogue is of utmost importance. 'I' statements promote empathy, understanding, and mutual respect. They encourage individuals to express their perspectives without instigating defensiveness or hostility in the other party. By saying "I feel...", you allow for the exploration of diverse perspectives and experiences, fostering an inclusive space for dialogue.

However, while 'I' statements can be transformative, their implementation is not an automatic guarantee of productive conversations. It requires genuine introspection and a commitment to express oneself honestly and respectfully. As such, these statements should always be used thoughtfully and sincerely. When used correctly, 'I' statements can significantly enhance DEI conversations, facilitating greater understanding, fostering respect, and promoting the harmonious exchange of ideas and experiences.

Without a doubt, incorporating "I" statements in our dialogue is an influential technique that fosters respectful and meaningful DEI discussions. Let's delve deeper into why this is crucial:

1. **Upholds Personal Accountability:** Utilizing "I" statements empowers us to claim our thoughts and feelings, steering clear of the blame game. This strategy promotes accountability for our emotional reactions and shifts the dynamic of the conversation toward a more personal and responsible direction.

2. **Circumvents Confrontation:** When we lead our sentences with "you," it can inadvertently appear confrontational, putting the other person in a defensive position. In contrast, "I" statements articulate our experiences without attributing blame, allowing for a more balanced exchange.

3. **Facilitates Empathy:** Articulating feelings and experiences through "I" statements offers an invitation to the other person to step into our shoes, fostering a sense of empathy. This empathetic understanding can pave the way to mutual respect and shared perspectives.

4. **Enables Open Discussion:** "I" statements, by their very nature, promote a receptive listening environment, helping the other person grasp our viewpoint more readily. This open-hearted sharing kindles honest, productive, and meaningful DEI dialogues.

To put it into perspective, consider this example: instead of expressing, "You're sidelining the significance of diversity," a more constructive approach would be to say, "I feel anxious that we might be overlooking the criticality of diversity." By doing so, we center the conversation on the issue at hand, avoiding it from spiraling into a personal disagreement.

Be Transparent

Transparency and openness are fundamental to fostering meaningful and productive DEI (Diversity, Equity, and Inclusion) conversations. Here's why:

1. **Promotes Authenticity:** When you're transparent and open about your experiences, you allow others to see your authentic self. This authenticity can build trust and rapport, making it easier to engage in meaningful discussions about sensitive topics.

2. **Encourages Empathy:** Sharing your experiences openly can help others empathize with your perspective. This empathy can lead to a deeper understanding and mutual respect, which are vital in DEI conversations.

3. **Challenges Stereotypes and Biases:** Openly discussing your personal experiences can challenge stereotypes and biases, contributing to a broader understanding of diversity and inclusion.

4. **Creates a Safe Space:** When you're open about your experiences, including the hard things, it signals to others that it's okay to do the same. This can create a safe space for everyone to share their experiences and feelings, fostering a more inclusive and supportive environment.

5. **Facilitates Learning and Growth:** Transparency and openness can lead to learning and growth, both for you and for the people you're engaging with. By sharing your experiences, you provide others with the opportunity to learn from your perspective, and vice versa.

Remember, DEI conversations can often be challenging and uncomfortable. But it's in this discomfort that growth can occur. By being transparent and open, you can contribute to a more understanding, inclusive, and equitable society.

A JOHN STORY: In a recent Diversity, Equity, and Inclusion (DEI) dialogue we were having at a pretty large multi-state company, there was a remarkable breakthrough that underscored the power of transparency. A senior executive, who had always maintained a staunch, unemotional facade, surprised everyone by sharing her personal experiences with discrimination. The room fell silent as she unfolded her stories of hardship and the struggles, she faced climbing the corporate ladder due to her ethnicity. Her raw and genuine sharing shattered the perceived barriers between her and the rest of the team, fostering a deep connection and empathy among them. This unexpected transparency sparked a chain reaction, prompting others to share their own experiences with diverse challenges, leading to a transformative and profoundly rich conversation. It was a powerful testament to the fact that when we strip away pretense and openly share our vulnerabilities and experiences, we open doors to understanding and mutual respect, pivotal elements in a successful DEI conversation.

Note: There is so much value and love hiding underneath the veil of professionalism, we must unveil ourselves to connect more deeply with those in our corner of the world.

Passive Aggressive Is Aggressive

Often when we say passive it kind of softens the punch of an aggressive behavior but the fact is passive aggressive is aggressive. Passive aggression is taken to heart deeper than somebody punching us or kicking us. We can feel it in our soul. It is so important to make sure that we are not being passive-aggressive in our delivery because we feel as though we are not able to say the things we want to say. So, we'll find sarcastic or shady useless nice ways of delivering comments to somebody with the intent of getting their attention and the lack of concern for how it's going to make them feel. That

Step 2 – NO OFFENSE

lack of concern over us wanting to move people in a direction without being overtly loud angry or belligerent still holds the same amount of aggression to them and as we are aware, it should be eliminated from our repertoire. Passive aggression is also manipulation and nobody wants to be a manipulator. Be a leader a lover and a lifter of people.

Passive-aggressive behavior, while often subtle and indirect, can be just as damaging as overt aggression in DEI (Diversity, Equity, and Inclusion) conversations. This is due to several reasons:

1. **Dismissal of Experiences and Perspectives:** Passive-aggressive behaviors, such as eye-rolling, sighing, or sarcastic comments, can send a message that the speaker's experiences or perspectives are invalid or unimportant. This can discourage open dialogue and create an environment where certain voices are silenced.

2. **Creates an Unsafe Space:** DEI conversations require a safe, respectful space where individuals feel comfortable sharing their experiences and perspectives. Passive-aggressive behavior can create an uncomfortable and hostile environment, making individuals less likely to participate and share their stories.

3. **Undermines Trust and Respect:** Trust and respect are crucial for productive DEI conversations. Passive-aggressive behavior can undermine these elements, leading to a lack of genuine engagement and understanding.

4. **Avoids Authentic Dialogue:** Passive-aggressive behavior often avoids direct confrontation and honest communication. This avoidance can prevent the necessary, sometimes difficult, conversations that need to occur for true understanding and progress in DEI. Many people spent a good chunk of their lives avoiding confrontation and some of it using passive-aggressive behavior. We are all a work in progress, but don't be afraid to put in the dialogue to create progress.

5. **Perpetuates Inequities:** Passive-aggressive responses to DEI conversations can perpetuate systemic inequities by dismissing or trivializing the experiences of marginalized groups. This can hinder progress toward greater equity and inclusion.

In essence, passive-aggressive behavior can derail DEI conversations and prevent the growth and understanding these conversations aim to achieve. It's essential to promote open, respectful, and

Step 2 – NO OFFENSE

authentic dialogue when discussing DEI topics to create a more inclusive and equitable environment.

Fairytale in a Land Far, Far Away: In the vibrant town of Unityville, a diverse group of people thrived. Known for its annual Unity Day celebration, this year, the city council added a DEI (Diversity, Equity, and Inclusion) forum. Anticipation filled the air as townsfolk congregated for the forum.

One of the residents, Emily, a woman of color, mustered courage and shared her encounters with implicit bias in Unityville. As she spoke, she noticed another townsperson, Tom, showing signs of dismissive behavior, like rolling his eyes and whispering sarcastic comments. Emily, feeling invalidated, decided to have a conversation with Tom post-forum.

She gracefully used the three easy steps to having a Dei conversation; feeling fully equipped, she engaged him. She asked questions and listened and was able to learn more about Tom and also vulnerably and transparently share how she felt about the nonchalant actions were a form of aggression and had impacted her and the overall discussion. Tom, taken aback, apologized, promising to improve, and was thankful that someone talked to him because he didn't really realize that he wasn't being the person he thought he was inside. This incident marked a profound change in Tom and Unityville's conversations around DEI.

For videos and more demonstrations of these conversations, please visit our website at johnemays.com. Here, you will find practical examples illustrating how these discussions can be conducted in real-life situations.

Addressing Misunderstandings

A misunderstanding is a situation where someone interprets words or actions incorrectly. Such situations can be quite common, especially in conversations around Diversity, Equity, and Inclusion (DEI), where many people may struggle to understand or interpret the emotions, words, and actions of others effectively. Understanding body language can be helpful, but in DEI contexts, body language can often lead to more misunderstandings. This is particularly true when people are feeling vulnerable, sensitive, or find themselves at a loss for words.

Feeling unheard can also make people less comprehensible. When people are experiencing strong emotions, the risk of misunderstandings can rise. It's our responsibility to be aware of this, to try

Step 2 – NO OFFENSE

and minimize misunderstandings from the onset, and to be prepared to address them when they do occur. It's essential not to shy away from or avoid these misunderstandings, but to confront them head-on, as this is a crucial step towards better understanding and effective communication in DEI conversations.

Addressing misunderstandings in Diversity, Equity, and Inclusion (DEI) conversations is vital for several reasons:

1. **Fosters Mutual Understanding:** DEI conversations involve diverse viewpoints based on different personal experiences and backgrounds. Misunderstandings are common and addressing them promotes mutual understanding and respect.

2. **Avoids Escalation:** Unaddressed misunderstandings can escalate into conflicts, derail the conversation, and potentially harm relationships. By addressing misunderstandings promptly, we can maintain a constructive and respectful dialogue.

3. **Builds Trust:** Openly addressing and resolving misunderstandings demonstrates transparency and honesty, key elements in building trust among participants.

4. **Promotes Learning:** Every misunderstanding is a learning opportunity. It allows participants to broaden their perspectives and deepen their understanding of diverse experiences and viewpoints.

Here's how to address misunderstandings in DEI conversations:

1. **Active Listening:** Pay full attention to the speaker. Listen not only to their words, but also observe their body language, tone of voice, and emotions. This will help you understand their perspective better and spot any potential misunderstandings.

2. **Seek Clarification:** If you're unsure about what the other person means, ask for clarification. It's better to ask and understand correctly than to assume and misunderstand.

3. **Express Yourself Clearly:** Be clear and precise about your thoughts and feelings. Use 'I' statements to express your viewpoint without blaming or accusing.

4. **Apologize if Needed:** If a misunderstanding has led to upset or offense, don't hesitate to apologize. An honest apology can go a long way in mending bridges and rebuilding trust.

5. **Be Patient:** Resolving misunderstandings takes time and patience. Allow each person the time they need to express their views and feelings.

Remember, the goal of DEI conversations is to promote understanding, respect, and inclusion. Addressing misunderstandings is a vital part of this process.

A JOHN STORY:

As the head of Equity and Inclusion for a multinational corporation, I have always taken great pride in promoting unity and understanding in our diverse workforce. However, even in this role, I once found myself facing an unexpected allegation of disrespecting a particular community.

It was after a large company gathering that a staff member, Anna, approached me. I immediately sensed her unease as she opened the conversation. "John," she said, "I feel that you intentionally neglected our Jewish community by overlooking the celebration of Yom Kippur, a significant holiday in our faith. For a DEI executive, this seems quite a mistake."

Taken aback, I carefully considered her words. Although surprised, I thanked her for her courage in voicing her concern. "Anna," I replied, "I'm grateful you've come forward. I assure you it wasn't my intention to overlook or exclude anyone. My role is to encourage inclusivity, not division."

I invited Anna into my office for a more in-depth conversation. As we sat down, I focused on listening to her. As she shared her disappointment and the importance of Yom Kippur, I became aware of my oversight. This conversation gave me a chance to learn more about the Jewish traditions and holidays.

Sincerely apologizing to Anna, I explained the oversight was unintentional. "I'm sorry for the misunderstanding, Anna. Thank you for bringing this to my attention. Going forward, we'll ensure that we not only recognize but also honor Yom Kippur and other significant holidays for all cultures within our company," I promised.

Anna seemed reassured by my words, feeling heard and respected. She understood that even within DEI, mistakes can happen. What mattered was the willingness to learn, correct, and move forward.

In an inspiring turn of events, Anna became an active advocate for our DEI initiatives. She began participating enthusiastically in various DEI programs, inspiring others in her community to do the same.

Step 2 – NO OFFENSE

This incident proved to be a powerful lesson for me, Anna, and our entire company. It reinforced the value of understanding and respecting diversity. It also set us on the path for an even more effective DEI program, making us all more aware and appreciative of the diverse cultures within our organization.

Step 3 – NO PENALTIES

You're on the precipice of unlocking phenomenal DEI conversations anywhere, anytime, with anybody. The third, and arguably most crucial component to ensuring enduring success and resilience in these dialogues is the principle of "No Penalties".

When we say, "No Penalties", we imply a commitment to creating an aftermath of these conversations that is free from lingering emotional and psychological strains. It means ensuring that these exchanges are safe and fulfilling, whether they occur amongst peers, within families, or in professional environments. It means leaving the person you converse with feeling whole, uplifted, and better equipped to navigate their world.

To live up to this commitment, we must let go of grudges and resist the temptation to assume that others may bear grudges against us. The fear and actuality of retaliation are barriers to the open and productive discourse we seek in DEI conversations.

Remember, the purpose of any conversation is to influence and inspire change - in others, as well as ourselves. This can only occur in an environment of

Step 3 – NO PENALTIES

mutual respect and understanding. Thus, it is paramount that we safeguard the reputation of others and confine the conversation to its intended context.

Everyone involved in these discussions should feel free to express their thoughts without fearing that each word might be used against them. Similarly, you should not bear the burden of constantly second-guessing your own words. Such fears can deter you from future conversations, leading to burnout and counteracting the very purpose of these discussions.

So, how do we ensure DEI conversations free from penalties? We start by letting go of self-judgment and avoiding the judgment of others. We cultivate trustworthiness, maintain confidentiality, and embrace vulnerability, creating a psychologically safe environment.

The triumvirate of mutuality, confidentiality, and transparency are vital keys to fostering an ongoing, transformative DEI discourse.

Remember not to penalize yourself. The worst penalties are the penalties we impose upon ourselves. It takes inward grace to show external grace. We must understand that for many of us it will require a good deal of effort and practice and you will need to understand that the process may take some time for some. Give yourself some grace and don't get discouraged, especially if you are working on some long-ingrained habits. Success is in the journey!

By getting a hold of these, you have the potential to spark the changes you desire. In doing so, you can catalyze a wave of influential, productive DEI conversations that ripple through your circle of influence and beyond. Together, let's create a more understanding, equitable, and inclusive world.

Amazing Grace

It's important to recognize the power of grace as a guiding principle. Grace represents a divine gift of love, forgiveness, and benevolence. By embodying grace in these conversations, we show love and understanding toward people who are different from us. We forgive any misunderstandings or missteps, and we actively seek to do good for others. We listen with empathy and respond with respect, acknowledging the inherent worth and dignity of each person, no matter their race, religion, gender, or any other distinguishing characteristic. We strive to create an environment where everyone feels safe, seen, and valued, reflecting love for all of humanity.

Step 3 – NO PENALTIES

Furthermore, grace calls us to approach DEI conversations with humility and openness. This means admitting when we don't understand or when we've made a mistake and seeking to learn from those experiences. It means being patient, not just with others, but with ourselves, as we navigate these complex issues. By demonstrating grace, we acknowledge that progress takes time and that everyone is on their own unique journey toward understanding and acceptance. We become catalysts for positive change, fostering an environment of growth and inclusivity. When we let grace guide our DEI conversations, we're not just talking about diversity, equity, and inclusion - we're living it.

Showing grace in DEI (Diversity, Equity, and Inclusion) conversations is vital and can be transformative for several reasons:

1. **Promotes Understanding:** Grace allows us to approach misunderstandings and missteps with patience and a willingness to educate rather than blame. It fosters an environment where individuals can learn from each other and deepen their understanding of complex DEI issues.

2. **Encourages Openness:** When we show grace, we create a space where people feel safe to

express their thoughts, questions, and even their doubts or misgivings. This openness is crucial in DEI conversations where individuals need to explore uncomfortable and challenging topics.

3. **Fosters Respect:** Showing grace often means respecting the experiences and viewpoints of others, even when they differ from our own. It encourages mutual respect, a key element in successful DEI conversations.

4. **Builds Trust:** By demonstrating grace, we show that we are willing to listen, learn, and grow together. This can build trust among participants, making them more comfortable sharing their experiences and insights.

5. **Supports Personal Growth:** DEI conversations often involve personal growth and change. Showing grace acknowledges that everyone is at a different stage in their DEI journey. It supports a growth mindset, where mistakes are seen as opportunities to learn and improve, rather than as failures.

6. **Strengthens Relationships:** Grace helps to maintain and strengthen relationships, even when conversations become difficult. By extending grace, we can navigate conflicts and

disagreements in a way that preserves and enhances the relationship.

Remember, showing grace doesn't mean avoiding hard conversations or ignoring harmful behavior. Rather, it's about approaching these issues with empathy, patience, and a shared commitment to growth and understanding.

No Cancel Rule - Don't Cancel Anyone

The concept of "canceling" or "cancel culture" typically involves public criticism and boycott of individuals (often celebrities or public figures) who have said or done something considered offensive or unacceptable. The act of canceling can be a powerful way for marginalized communities to hold individuals accountable for their actions and to demand change.

In environments composed of diverse groups of individuals representing a multitude of perspectives, the fear of "walking on eggshells" can often pose a significant challenge in DEI (Diversity, Equity, and Inclusion) conversations. Many individuals fear participating due to the risk of "cancel culture," a social phenomenon where a person faces public criticism and ostracism due to perceived offensive actions or statements. Leaders, in particular, may choose to avoid these conversations rather than risk potential backlash, negative publicity, or damaging their personal brand.

Therefore, it is essential, a priority or "action item number one" to establish a no-cancel rule in DEI discussions. This rule encourages respect for differing viewpoints and safeguards the reputations and personal brands of participants. The rule implies that if you truly care about understanding someone and their perspective, it's vital to respect and protect their reputation. After all, what you project and condone eventually comes back to you - if you propagate cancel culture, you may, in turn, be "canceled." Therefore, it's vital to establish a psychologically safe space in DEI conversations, ensuring that the fear of cancellation does not obstruct open and sincere dialogue.

And certainly, in the context of DEI (Diversity, Equity, and Inclusion) conversations, especially within personal or professional environments, avoiding "canceling" is crucial for several reasons:

1. **Promotes Dialogue and Learning:** DEI conversations are intended to be spaces for growth, learning, and increased understanding. Canceling someone can shut down this dialogue, preventing both personal growth and collective

progress toward greater understanding and inclusivity.

2. **Encourages Openness:** Fear of being canceled can create a culture of silence and fear, where individuals are afraid to participate in DEI conversations, ask questions, or express their thoughts. This can prevent meaningful engagement in DEI initiatives.

3. **Respects Human Complexity:** People are complex and multi-faceted, capable of change and growth. Canceling someone does not allow for the possibility of learning, growth, and change.

4. **Fosters Empathy and Compassion:** Cancel culture often lacks compassion and understanding. In DEI conversations, it's important to approach each other with empathy and compassion, recognizing that everyone is at a different stage in their DEI journey.

5. **Supports Accountability:** Canceling can lead to avoidance of accountability. Instead, constructive feedback and restorative practices encourage individuals to acknowledge their mistakes, learn from them, and make amends.

Remember, the goal of DEI conversations is to promote understanding, inclusivity, and equity. A culture that avoids canceling and instead focuses on learning, growth, and accountability can better support these objectives.

Personal Confidentiality

Confidentiality is a cornerstone of trust, particularly in DEI (Diversity, Equity, and Inclusion) conversations. These conversations often involve sharing personal experiences, feelings, and perspectives on sensitive topics related to race, gender, religion, culture, and other aspects of identity. Participants need to feel secure that what they share will be respected and kept confidential. If this trust is broken, it can significantly damage the open and honest dialogue that these discussions depend upon, and individuals may become reluctant to share in the future.

There are a few key ways to foster and maintain confidentiality in DEI conversations:

1. **Establish Clear Guidelines:** From the outset, make it clear that confidentiality is expected. This includes not only not sharing the personal stories and experiences others disclose but also not revealing who participated in the conversation.

2. **Respect Boundaries:** Encourage everyone to respect each other's boundaries. This means not

Step 3 – NO PENALTIES

pressuring anyone to share more than they are comfortable with and honoring the privacy of others.

3. **Foster a Safe Environment:** Work to create a safe and supportive environment where people feel comfortable sharing their experiences and perspectives. This includes setting a tone of respect and understanding and taking steps to address any behavior that threatens this environment.

4. **Ensure Confidentiality in Follow-Ups:** If there are any follow-up actions or discussions stemming from the DEI conversation, ensure they also honor confidentiality. For example, if a broader organizational change is suggested, the proposal should be made in a way that doesn't attribute it to any specific individual or reveal any private conversations.

5. **Provide Confidential Channels:** If individuals want to continue the conversation or raise specific issues in a more private setting, provide channels for them to do so confidentially, such as private meetings or an anonymous suggestion box.

By upholding confidentiality, you demonstrate respect for each person's experiences and foster an environment where trust can flourish. Obviously, if you both agree for some or part of your conversation or some key ah-ha moment happens and you both feel comfortable, then share away, other than that, keep it tight and maintain the integrity of trust. This in turn can lead to more open, meaningful, and productive DEI conversations when established as a rule or non-negotiable value.

Confidentiality as a rule has several important functions:

1. **Builds Trust:** Knowing that their thoughts, experiences, and feelings will not be shared without their permission can make individuals more comfortable and willing to participate in DEI conversations.

2. **Promotes Openness and Honesty:** When participants know their words won't be shared outside the conversation, they may be more likely to express their honest thoughts, feelings, and experiences, which can lead to more authentic and productive conversations.

3. **Protects Privacy:** Some DEI topics can be personal and sensitive. The Confidentiality Rule helps to respect and protect participants' privacy.

4. **Prevents Misinterpretation:** Sharing parts of the conversation out of context can lead to

misunderstandings and misinterpretations. Confidentiality can prevent this.

However, it's important to clarify the boundaries of this rule. For example, if a participant reveals they're planning to harm themselves or others, or if they disclose information about illegal activities, confidentiality may need to be broken for safety or legal reasons. These exceptions should be clearly communicated to participants before DEI conversations begin.

And as always, this rule should not be used to shield or ignore harmful behavior. If someone behaves inappropriately or disrespectfully during a DEI conversation, that behavior should be addressed appropriately within the given context, keeping in mind the privacy and safety of all participants.

Following Up on Difficult Conversations

Not to be poetic, but we need to understand that the strength of a DEI conversation lies not in its comfort, but in its challenge. It is through navigating the varying terrain of our differences that we discover the common ground of our shared humanity.

Following up on difficult DEI conversations is of utmost importance because it serves as an affirmation that the conversation was not a mere formality, but a genuine attempt to address and remedy any issues or disparities. A follow-up shows participants that their voices were heard, their concerns acknowledged, and that the topics they shared are taken seriously. It's an act of accountability, displaying commitment to the ongoing process of fostering diversity, equity, and inclusion. Moreover, it helps build trust and credibility, as it demonstrates that the organization or individuals involved are sincerely dedicated to progress and change. Without a proper follow-up, participants might feel their efforts and emotional labor were in vain, undermining the progress made during the conversation.

Therefore, a consistent follow-up is crucial to the overall success and integrity of DEI conversations. These discussions often delve into deeply personal experiences, societal issues, and complex concepts. Therefore, navigating such conversations can be challenging and potentially fraught with misunderstanding or misinterpretation. Here's how to effectively follow up:

1. **Summarize Key Points:** After a DEI conversation, summarizing the key points can provide a clear record of what was discussed. This might include the main ideas, shared experiences, or differing

viewpoints that emerged. This summary should be as objective as possible to ensure that everyone feels their views and experiences were accurately represented.

2. **Clarify Agreements:** DEI conversations may lead to new understandings, decisions, or plans for action. It's important to clearly state any agreements or decisions that were made, to ensure everyone is on the same page moving forward.

3. **Check in on Emotions:** DEI conversations can evoke strong emotions. Following up with individuals to check in on how they're feeling after the discussion can show empathy and care and provide an opportunity to address any residual emotional issues or concerns.

4. **Provide Next Steps:** If the conversation led to plans for future action, these should be clearly stated in the follow-up. This might include further conversations, policy changes, training sessions, or individual actions that participants have committed to.

5. **Open the Door for Further Conversation:** Allow for the possibility that participants may need time to process the conversation and may have

additional thoughts, questions, or concerns later. Make it clear that further discussion is welcome and that the conversation about DEI is ongoing.

Following up in these ways shows your commitment to the DEI process. It helps to ensure that everyone feels heard, understood, and clear about the outcome of the conversation and the next steps. It also helps to build trust and openness, which are crucial for effective DEI conversations.

The Challenge- Equity and Inclusion Begins and Ends with You

Now, we've reached a really important part of our journey. It's time to switch gears from just learning about Diversity, Equity, and Inclusion (DEI) to actually doing something about it. You see, if you've got a bag full of knowledge and don't share it or use it, it's like having a basket of fresh fruits and not eating them. They're of no use unless they're shared and enjoyed.

Remember, the journey of DEI starts with you It can really make a difference. But it can also stop with you if we don't use or share what we've learned. So, we need to push ourselves to not just understand this important stuff but to actually do something with it.

Step 3 – NO PENALTIES

So, here's a challenge for you. This is your moment to shine and make a real difference. You've got the tools, the knowledge, and the power to improve things. It's up to you to carry the torch and keep the conversation about DEI going.

Let's step up to this challenge. Let's show the world how personal responsibility can move DEI forward. It's not someone else's job; it's ours. And it starts with one small step. You've got this! Go out there and make a difference!

But the journey doesn't stop there. It's not just about understanding DEI, it's about becoming a doer. You've listened and learned, now it's time to put all that into action. Here's a fun and meaningful challenge to help you become a DEI doer:

The DEI Action Challenge:

1. **Look Around:** Look at your life—your work, your friends, the places you hang out online. Where could things be more diverse, fair, and inclusive? Find at least three areas where you could help make things better.

2. **Start Conversations:** Once you've found those areas, it's time to start talking. Remember, these talks should be friendly and respectful. You're not

trying to win an argument; you're just sharing ideas.

3. **Make a Plan:** Now that you've talked about it, what can you do to help? Maybe you can share resources, speak up for others, or make sure everyone feels welcome. Make a list of things you can do to promote DEI.

4. **Keep Yourself on Track:** Write down your goals and the steps you're going to take to reach them. Check in on your progress every now and then. If you hit a roadblock, figure out how to get around it.

5. **Share Your Journey:** Tell others about what you're doing. You might inspire them to become DEI doers too. Share your wins and your struggles—it's all part of the journey.

6. **Cheer Others On:** Encourage others to become DEI doers. Share this challenge with them and offer your support as they start their own DEI journey.

Remember, this isn't about being perfect. It's about making a positive change, step by step. Even small actions can make a big difference if we keep at it. Now, it's your turn to step into the game. You're ready for this!

Step 3 – NO PENALTIES

In the end, making our world a more equitable and inclusive place is up to us. Each one of us plays a vital role in making that happen. Let's take up this challenge and step boldly into a brighter future. You've got this!

Appendix

Sure, here's an alphabetical list of some of the most common diversity terminology:

- **Accessibility:** The design of products, devices, services, or environments for people with disabilities.
- **Ableism:** Discrimination and social prejudice against people with disabilities.
- **Affinity Bias:** The tendency to gravitate towards people who are most like us.
- **Ageism:** Discrimination or prejudice against individuals based on their age.
- **Allyship:** The active, consistent, and arduous practice of unlearning and re-evaluating beliefs and actions, in which a person seeks to work in solidarity with a marginalized individual or group of people.
- **BIPOC:** Stands for Black, Indigenous, People of Color.
- **Bias:** An inclination or prejudice for or against one person or group, especially in a way considered to be unfair.

Appendix

- **Bicultural:** Identifying with the cultures of two different ethnic, national, or language groups.

- **Bisexual:** An individual who is physically, romantically, and/or emotionally attracted to both men and women.

- **CEI:** Chief Equity and Inclusion. This is a role in some organizations, similar to a Chief Diversity Officer.

- **Classism:** Discrimination based on social class or economic status.

- **Cisgender:** A term for people whose gender identity matches their sex assigned at birth.

- **Cultural Competence:** The ability to understand, communicate with, and effectively interact with people across cultures.

- **DEI:** Diversity, Equity, and Inclusion. This is a common acronym in workplaces and education that stresses the importance of diverse identities, fair treatment, and inclusive environments.

- **DEIA:** Diversity, Equity, Inclusion, and Accessibility. This is similar to IDEA but with a different order.

- **DEIB:** Diversity, Equity, Inclusion, and Belonging. This acronym extends DEI by emphasizing that people should not only be included but also feel a sense of belonging.

- **DEIBJ:** Diversity, Equity, Inclusion, Belonging, and Justice. This extends DEIB by including the idea of social justice or fair treatment of all people.
- **Diversity:** Variety in the identity experiences of people, including race, ethnicity, gender, age, national origin, religion, disability, sexual orientation, socioeconomic status, education, marital status, language, and physical appearance.
- **E:** Usually stands for Equity in the context of DEI.
- **EB:** Equity and Belonging. This acronym focuses on fair treatment and the feeling of belonging.
- **EIB:** Equity, Inclusion, and Belonging. This is a variant of DEIB, focusing on fair treatment, inclusive environments, and a sense of belonging without explicitly mentioning diversity.
- **Equity:** The fair treatment, access, opportunity, and advancement for all people.
- **Ethnocentrism:** Evaluation of other cultures according to the preconceptions originating in the standards and customs of one's own culture.
- **Gender Expression:** The way in which a person expresses their gender identity, typically through their appearance, dress, and behavior.

Appendix

- **Gender Identity:** A personal conception of oneself as male, female, both, and neither.

- **Heterosexism:** Discrimination or prejudice against homosexuals on the assumption that heterosexuality is the norm.

- **Homophobia:** Fear, hatred, discomfort with, or mistrust of people who are lesbian, gay, or bisexual.

- **IDEA:** Inclusion, Diversity, Equity, and Accessibility. This is similar to DEIA but with a different order.

- **IE:** Inclusion and Equity. A variant of EI, focuses on inclusive environments and fair treatment.

- **Inclusion:** The act of creating environments in which any individual or group can feel welcomed, respected, supported, and valued.

- **Intersectionality:** The complex, cumulative way in which the effects of different forms of discrimination (such as racism, sexism, and classism) combine, overlap, or intersect.

- **JEDI:** Justice, Equity, Diversity, and Inclusion. This acronym includes a focus on justice as well as diversity, equity, and inclusion.

- **LGBTQ+IA:** Stands for lesbian, gay, bisexual, transgender, queer/questioning, intersex, and asexual.

- **Microaggressions:** Everyday verbal, nonverbal, and environmental slights, snubs, or insults, whether intentional or unintentional, which communicate hostile, derogatory, or negative messages to target persons based solely upon their marginalized group membership.

- **Neurodiversity:** The concept that people with neurological differences like autism, ADHD, and dyslexia should be respected and recognized as naturally occurring variations within the human species.

- **Non-binary:** An umbrella term for people who don't identify as only male or only female.

- **Privilege:** Unearned social advantages, benefits, or degrees of prestige and respect that an individual has by virtue of belonging to certain social identity groups.

- **Queer:** A term for people who are not heterosexual and/or cisgender. Previously used as a derogatory term, it is now reclaimed and used as an umbrella term within the LGBTQ+ community.

- **Racism:** Prejudice, discrimination, or antagonism directed against a person or people on the basis of their membership in a particular racial or ethnic group.

Appendix

- **READI:** Respect, Equity, Accessibility, Diversity, and Inclusion. This acronym extends DEI by adding respect and accessibility to the mix.

- **REDI:** Racial Equity, Diversity, and Inclusion. This acronym specifically highlights racial equity as part of the larger diversity and inclusion initiative.

- **Sexism:** Prejudice, stereotyping, or discrimination on the basis of sex.

- **Stereotype:** A widely held but oversimplified image or idea of a particular type of person or thing.

- **Transgender:** An umbrella term for people whose gender identity differs from the sex they were assigned at birth.

- **Unconscious Bias:** Also known as implicit bias, it refers to a bias that we are unaware of, and which happens outside of our control. It is a bias that happens automatically and is triggered by our brain making quick judgments and assessments of people and situations.

- **Xenophobia:** Dislike of or prejudice against people from other countries.

Remember, all these acronyms refer to the principles of creating a diverse and inclusive environment where everyone is treated fairly and feels like they belong. The specific choice of acronym may reflect an organization's particular emphasis or approach.

AI BONUS SECTION

Diversity, equity, and inclusion (DEI) is a critical issue for businesses of all sizes. A diverse workforce is more innovative, more creative, and more profitable. However, creating a truly inclusive workplace is a challenge.

One of the biggest challenges to DEI is unconscious bias. Unconscious bias is the tendency to make decisions based on our own personal experiences and beliefs, without even realizing it. This can lead to discrimination against people of different races, genders, sexual orientations, and other identities.

AI can help to level the playing field in DEI conversations by identifying and addressing unconscious bias. AI can be used to analyze data and identify patterns that may indicate unconscious bias. This information can then be used to educate employees about unconscious bias and how to mitigate it.

AI can also be used to create more inclusive workplaces. For example, AI can be used to develop hiring algorithms that are less likely to discriminate against people of color or women. AI can also be used to create training programs that help employees understand and appreciate the value of diversity.

AI is a powerful tool that can be used to level the playing field in DEI conversations. By using AI, businesses can create more diverse, equitable, and inclusive workplaces.

Here are some specific examples of how AI is being used to improve DEI:

- **Hiring:** AI is being used to develop hiring algorithms that are less likely to discriminate against people of color or women. For example, IBM's AI-powered hiring tool, called HireVue, uses video interviews to assess candidates. HireVue has been shown to be more accurate than traditional hiring methods at identifying top performers, and it is also less likely to discriminate against people of color or women.

- **Promotions:** AI is being used to identify employees who are ready for promotions. For example, Workday's AI-powered promotion tool, called People Insights, uses data to identify employees who are performing well and who have the potential for advancement. People Insights has been shown to be more accurate than traditional promotion methods at identifying high-performing employees.

- **Training:** AI is being used to create training programs that help employees understand and appreciate the value of diversity. For example, Google's AI-powered training program, called Retraining AI, teaches employees about unconscious bias and how to mitigate it. Retraining AI has been shown to be effective at reducing unconscious bias among employees.

These are just a few examples of how AI is being used to improve DEI. As AI continues to develop, it is likely that we will see even more innovative and effective ways to use AI to create more diverse, equitable, and inclusive workplaces.

One of the threats of AI on DEI:

- AI can perpetuate bias. AI systems are trained on data, and if that data is biased, the AI system will be biased as well. This can lead to AI systems making decisions that discriminate against certain groups of people.

- AI can be used to automate tasks that are currently done by people of color and women. This could lead to job losses and increased unemployment among these groups.

- AI can be used to create new forms of discrimination. For example, AI could be used to create facial recognition software that is less accurate for people of color. This could lead to people of color being stopped and searched by the police more often.

- AI can be used to create echo chambers. AI systems can be used to recommend content that is similar to what people have already seen. This could lead to people being exposed to only information that confirms their existing biases.

It is important to be aware of these threats so that we can take steps to mitigate them. We need to make sure that AI systems are trained on data that is as diverse as possible. We also need to develop policies and regulations that will prevent AI from being used to discriminate against certain groups of people.

Here are some things that can be done to mitigate the threats of AI on DEI:

- Be intentional about diversity and inclusion in the development of AI systems. This includes ensuring that the data used to train AI systems is diverse and that the people developing AI systems are representative of the populations they are designed to serve.

- Create policies and regulations that will prevent AI from being used to discriminate against certain groups of people. These policies could include requirements for AI systems to be transparent and explainable, and for companies to be held accountable for the actions of their AI systems.

- Educate the public about the potential threats of AI on DEI. This will help people to be aware of the risks and to demand that companies take steps to mitigate them.

By taking these steps, we can help to ensure that AI is used to promote DEI, rather than to harm it.

Remember!

Listen without being defensive; speak without being offensive; and never penalize the perspective of others!

Follow More content like this or just connect with me on LinkedIn:

linkedin.com/in/john-mays-a5082a42

Visit my website johnemays.com

On this website we share live demonstrations of these world changing DEI conversations, please visit our website at johnemays.com. Here, you will find practical examples illustrating how these discussions can be conducted in real-life situations with anybody, anytime, anywhere.

God bless,

JM

John E. Mays
THE I BELIEVE I CAN MAN

Made in the USA
Columbia, SC
05 July 2023